THE ART OF BEING HUMAN

THE ART OF BEING HUMAN

*What "Old Books"
Can Tell Us
(And Warn Us)
About Living in the 21st Century*

BY MICHAEL S. ROSE

Angelico Press

For information, address:
Angelico Press, Ltd.
169 Monitor St.
Brooklyn, NY 11222
www.angelicopress.com

paper 978-1-62138-895-1
cloth 978-1-62138-896-8

Book and cover design
by Michael Schrauzer

DEDICATION

This volume is dedicated to the inaugural
faculty at Cincinnati Classical Academy,
whose dedication to the pursuit of
goodness, beauty, and truth in education
is on joyful display each and every day.

CONTENTS

INTRODUCTION: *Human Concerns*
Dignity, Rights, and Duties   1

PART ONE: *Promethean Pursuits*   11
Science, Hubris, & the God Complex

Frankenstein (1818)   13
MARY SHELLEY

"The Body Snatcher" (1884)   19
ROBERT LOUIS STEVENSON

Never Let Me Go (2005)   27
KAZUO ISHIGURO

The Constant Gardener (2001)   36
JOHN LE CARRÉ

"Markheim" (1885)   43
ROBERT LOUIS STEVENSON

The Tragical History of Doctor Faustus (c. 1592)   48
CHRISTOPHER MARLOWE

"Young Goodman Brown" (1835)   54
NATHANIEL HAWTHORNE

PART TWO: *Transhumanist Goals*
Perfection, Comfort, & Immortality   61

Brave New World (1932)   63
ALDOUS HUXLEY

Gulliver's Travels (1726)   70
JONATHAN SWIFT

"The Birth-mark" (1843)   77
NATHANIEL HAWTHORNE

That Hideous Strength (1945)   81
C.S. LEWIS

PART THREE: *Totalitarian Dreams*
Propaganda, Manipulation, & Control   91

Nineteen Eighty-Four (1949)   93
GEORGE ORWELL

"Politics and the English Language" (1946)   105
GEORGE ORWELL

Fahrenheit 451 (1953)   112
RAY BRADBURY

The Thanatos Syndrome (1987)   120
WALKER PERCY

The Wanting Seed (1962)   127
ANTHONY BURGESS

"William Wilson" (1839)   135
EDGAR ALLAN POE

Things Fall Apart (1958)   140
CHINUA ACHEBE

Human Concerns: Dignity, Rights, and Duties

*F*or the past fifteen years, I've had the pleasure of teaching British and American literature at three Catholic high schools, exploring with teenagers some of life's big questions: Who are we? Why are we here? How should we live? Where are we going, and how do we get there? During my early years of teaching, I quickly discovered that I needed to do much more than lay down the curriculum. I had to inspire and to motivate, to challenge the minds and fire the imaginations of the students who were entrusted to me. I felt called to broaden their spiritual lives and to increase their capacity for mutual and self-respect. I have been doing all this, albeit with varying degrees of success, through the study of great works of literature that speak to the human race on themes of universal importance and provide an introduction to the breadth of human concerns and human wisdom. Reading these great works not only promotes the understanding of ideas but offers sustenance for the spirit as well as the mind. In the words of Mortimer Adler, a reader "may be transported, enriched, beguiled, delighted, amused, consoled, ennobled; taken to new and wonderful places, some of which are pure invention; introduced to characters who may become lifelong companions; allowed to overhear conversations that say what no one has ever said before; invited to share feelings that deepen their own" (The Paideia Program, 65).

Adler believed, as I do, that the pleasures of reading are always enhanced by discussing what one has read. He, along with like-minded educators, developed what he called the Paideia Program. We can think of this as the Socratic method applied to carefully directed classroom discussions. It is this Socratic seminar style that I adapted to my classes as the primary method to discuss the "great ideas" of literature—ideas like good and evil; pleasure and pain; virtue and vice; democracy and despotism; war and peace; happiness, justice, and wisdom. I did not saddle students with textbook assignments that belabor historical context, the author's politics, and tedious interpretations of a work's literary significance. (Don't get me wrong: I always provided students with the appropriate background and context.) We simply read, annotated, analyzed, and discussed the works themselves, all in the context of the "great ideas." Those seminar discussions did not stagnate in the realm of emotionally driven reader response as if we were partaking in a book club *Kaffeeklatsch*. Rather, they were purposefully analytical in nature and focused directly on the narrative at hand. That may sound obvious to many, but I knew that the seminar discussions would only ever be as good as the students' reading of the text itself. And here's the most important point: My students *had* to read the works we studied—not in summaries from SparkNotes or Wikipedia. They were asked to read, to annotate, and to carefully prepare to actively participate in each seminar by responding to a set of well-organized prompts in addition to crafting their own analytical and interpretive questions pertaining to these "great ideas" we identified. In other words, my class was not centered on my lectures to them about the great works; I did not hold the expectation that they would parrot my thoughts and interpretations back to me. In my view, that's a pretty low-level educational endeavor that reduces the study of literature to box-checking and regurgitation. It doesn't even require actually reading the assigned books. It is a misguided approach that is more about indoctrination than true education and intellectual (or emotional, spiritual, cultural, etc.) formation. In my experience, few students are inspired by that parroting approach.

The richest of these Socratic seminar discussions took place in my AP English Literature and Composition classes when I was teaching at an all-boys Catholic school in Cincinnati. As you may imagine, literature is a hard sell to a 16-year-old boy in the best of times. Asking students to read and discuss and write about significant works of fiction may sometimes seem a fool's errand. Nevertheless, most of these young men took away enduring life lessons, not from listening to me lecture to them—yes, I did that at times—but from engaging in frank discussion with their peers under my guidance about "great ideas" that often related to a central question that all great literature explores in one way or another: What does it mean to be human?

Although I've taught a variety of novels, plays, poems, and short stories over the years—from Homer to Shakespeare to Tolkien—I found the most fruitful seminar discussions consistently centered on three British novels, taught in succession, one tied into the next: Mary Shelley's *Frankenstein*, Aldous Huxley's *Brave New World*, and George Orwell's *Nineteen Eighty-Four*. I linked these imaginative works together with *Our Posthuman Future*, Francis Fukuyama's prescient critical survey of the 21st-century biotechnology revolution—typically introducing Fukuyama's book (and related nonfiction material) between our readings of *Frankenstein* and *Brave New World*. Through the seminar discussions of these three novels, many students for the first time began to see the study of literature as relatable and relevant to their lives—not just because we routinely discussed how the literary themes of these novels manifest themselves in the real-world culture of the 21st century but because they related directly to who they are, what they care about, and how they ultimately want to (and should) interact with the world around them. From my perspective, this is what the study of literature should—ideally—always do.

Year after year, these students moved beyond an academic exercise to an intellectual adventure that engaged their minds and hearts, and it is instructive to note that they did this by studying "old books" rather than politically correct bestsellers from the 1980s or rap songs from 2018. "Relatability" is by no means synonymous with "contemporary" or with base elements of pop culture. These literary discussions of "old books" appealed to their intellect, their emotions, and their imagination. They raised questions about life and death—and the afterlife too. They encouraged analytical thinking and reasoning about morality. They tied into the wisdom of the ages that has helped transmit Western culture from one generation to the next. And because I was teaching in the context of a Catholic school, these discussions routinely probed the role of religion, faith, and God in daily life. In our seminars on *Brave New World,* for example, we discussed the underlying philosophies (consumerism, hedonism, communism, authoritarianism, etc.) that in any century will dehumanize us and lead us away from God and all that is truly good and beautiful, that will push man to question the value of human existence.

Because year after year my students generated so many questions to further explore regarding the great ideas of these three masterworks of the 19th and 20th centuries, I designed a senior year literature elective to enable them to continue to explore our conversations on human nature, human rights, and human dignity that we began in their junior year AP course. I called this new course "Science Fiction and the Moral Imagination." For students already familiar with the seminal works of Shelley, Huxley, and Orwell, I was providing an opportunity to intentionally drill down on some of the pressing moral and cultural issues facing us in the 21st century. Not by dissecting narratives of space exploration and alien invasions, which is what the mind often conjures when we hear the term "science fiction," but rather by focusing on works by authors who explore both our wildest dreams and our greatest fears for where technological advancement (and the attitudes associated with it) might lead us—for better or for worse. This oft-dismissed literary genre presents many opportunities to exercise the moral imagination through attempts to anticipate future technological developments and to explore both the benefits and the dangers of these developments. More importantly, this vein of science fiction—perhaps "speculative fiction" is a better term—provides fertile ground for exploring universal themes related to human nature. Indeed, "great" science fiction is fueled by the concerns of the day just as much as by the fantastic imaginings of the future. The golden age of science fiction that produced seminal works like *Brave New World* and Ray Bradbury's *Fahrenheit 451* has now become the age of science fact: The technologies envisioned in the past by authors like Huxley and Bradbury have become realities or promise to become so in the coming years.

I taught "Science Fiction and the Moral Imagination" as an interdisciplinary reading and writing course drawing upon imaginative literature, science, art, architecture, philosophy, and theology to explore timeless issues and themes pertaining to emerging digital technology and bio-technology—all relating back to the implications these have for both the human person and human society. I introduced three relatively contemporary novels (*The Thanatos Syndrome* by Walker Percy, *The Constant Gardener* by John le Carré, and *Never Let Me Go* by Kazuo Ishiguro) along with a selection of short stories, essays, and other classic novels from the likes of Nathaniel Hawthorne, Jonathan Swift, Ray Bradbury, and C. S. Lewis. This reading syllabus set the stage for our exploration of the advancement of science and technology. We routinely asked four important questions about the speculative technologies being dramatized in the stories: What are the purported benefits? What are the acknowledged drawbacks? What are possible unintended consequences? And what are the ethical and moral considerations involved in the application of this technology? All of these questions, of course, tie back into its effects on the human person. At the same time, we did not lose sight of the value of a pleasurable and edifying narrative. After all, it is through literature that we see these speculative technologies—whether it's the elixir of life in Hawthorne's "The Birth-mark" or designer babies in *Brave New World*—brought to life in human society and where we "experience" the benefits, drawbacks, and consequences.

Here's the primary reason this course was popular with high school students: We didn't just sit around discussing symbols and metaphors (which admittedly has its place in the study of literature); we analyzed and discussed the fiction we read in terms of 21st-century emerging real-world applications and concerns, particularly in these areas: the posthumanist and transhumanist movements, human genetic engineering, designer babies, human cloning, neuropharmacology, emerging digital technologies, medical advancements, surveillance systems, and artificial intelligence. The following provided the guiding questions for the course:

- What is human nature? What does it mean to be human?
- Do we have a right to manipulate human nature?
- When does one begin to be and cease to be human? When does a person go beyond being human? Is that even possible?
- What is human dignity? What are human rights?
- What are the consequences of today's biotechnology revolution and the advancement of emerging digital technologies, including artificial intelligence?

• What does contemporary and classic literature have to say about today's biotechnology revolution and other scientific experiments involving the human person?

• What can we learn from science fiction literature to help us live in the 21st century?

• How can our understanding help us innovate in response to an ever-changing world?

The Art of Being Human is, in part, a chronicle of the class discussions (and intellectual adventures) in these two courses. As such, this book seeks to provide some answers to these fascinating and important guiding questions. It also strives to provide some insight on how best to explore them as a life-long learner with a healthy curiosity about the world around you and a desire to learn more about the great patrimony of literature and how it relates directly to us and our understanding of the world, past and present.

As Huxley, Orwell, and Bradbury make clear in their prescient classics that I will discuss in this book, great literature is essential to the transmission of important aspects of culture from one generation to the next. What *Brave New World, Nineteen Eighty-Four,* and *Fahrenheit 451* all have in common is that books are simply absent from their imagined dystopian societies. The citizens of *Brave New World* are too busy amusing themselves to have any interest in reading books, great or otherwise; Huxley's One World government ingeniously controls the masses by providing instant gratification of sensory desires through mindless recreation, meaningless sex, and drug-induced "happiness." The intended consequences include a suppression of their innate curiosity about the world around them, so much so that even the idea of reading a book is seen as an outdated absurdity. In *Nineteen Eighty-Four,* Orwell's government takes a brutal, authoritarian approach: Propaganda and disinformation are the order of the day, and anything other than official government statements are forbidden to be either read or written; no one dares even look at a book for fear of being thrown into a windowless room and tortured. In *Fahrenheit 451*, Bradbury's world is peopled by firefighters who, rather than putting out fires, burn any and every book. The irony is, however, that the vast majority of its citizens, as in Huxley's dystopia, have no use for the written word: pervasive screen time has come to dominate all aspects of society, including formal education. It is further instructive to note that in each of these dystopian societies, the heroes rebel by way of the book: Huxley's John the Savage discovers William Shakespeare, Orwell's Winston Smith keeps a forbidden diary, and Bradbury's Guy Montag turns from burning books to reading them, including the Holy Bible. All three rebellions point to an enduring truth: Literature matters; great books are essential to civilization. A sad fact of our own day is that, although we have more books available to us than at any time in history, fewer and fewer people are reading great literature of universal import, distracted as we are by social media, news feeds, political sloganeering, podcasts, mindless commercial television, Netflix, live-streaming sports at all hours, and constant text messaging. Even many educators, those charged with the literary formation of the younger generation, often appear to have convinced themselves and their charges that we no longer have time or use for "old books." Newfangled educational theories often see little value in literature that communicates perennial truths. Instead, educators opt for emotion-driven explorations of race, ethnicity, and sexual identity, trendy books that are often made into Hollywood movies that ironically supplant the books they purport to represent: Angie Thomas's *The Hate U Give* (2017) is an excellent example.

One can be forgiven then for believing that great books from past and present are on their way out, that they may soon remain but a fringe element of society, entertainment for antiquarians. Before these books go, we ought to try to understand the tremendous impact and influence these great works have on us as individuals and as a society. Before they go, consider this: "Old books" allow us to learn about ourselves, to benefit from the insight of others, to explore other beliefs and cultures, to expand our grasp of the machinations of history, to encourage us to question accepted knowledge, to consider ethical complexities, to learn better ways to live, to refine our judgment, to develop empathy for others (especially those who are unlike us), and of course to be entertained.

Although *The Art of Being Human* isn't meant to be a general argument for reading old books or studying great literature, it is meant to give a specific example of the impact great literature can and does have, especially in the realm of the cautionary tale, in considering how we might learn from the past in order to inform our present decisions and plan for the future, all the while maintaining our humanity amid a dehumanizing world.

PART ONE

Promethean Pursuits

SCIENCE, HUBRIS, &
THE GOD COMPLEX

Frankenstein (1818)

MARY SHELLEY

*V*ictor Frankenstein witnesses two events early in his life that will lead to his tragic demise. At age fifteen, he beholds the destruction of an enormous oak in his back yard by the forces of nature. A lightning strike obliterates the tree before his very eyes, leaving nothing but a blasted stump. Like his historical contemporary Benjamin Franklin, Victor marvels at the power of electricity, wondering how he might harness this incredible power of nature. A few years later, just as Victor is about to depart for medical studies at the University of Ingolstadt in Germany, his mother dies of scarlet fever after selflessly nursing her adopted daughter Elizabeth back to health. The aggregate of these two seemingly disparate events is an obsession that will consume—literally—the rest of his life and just about everyone he loves.

Victor, as a protagonist, has few redeeming traits. Even apart from his unhealthy obsession with harnessing the powers of nature for his own purposes, Victor is rash, imprudent, morally blind, subject to violent passions, and above all has little respect for the human person. "The world was to me a secret which I desired to divine," Victor confesses after all is said and done. His Faustian thirst for knowledge leads him on a tragic quest to learn the "hidden laws of nature" and to unlock "the secrets of heaven." Victor explains that he will "pioneer a new way, explore unknown powers, and unfold to the world the deepest mysteries of creation."

That quest leads him at first to absorb the fancies of alchemists and astrologists like Paracelsus and Cornelius Agrippa, whose Gnosticism beguiles Victor. Unfortunately, his own intellectual impetuosity blinds him to the important fact that these Renaissance philosophers trafficked in the black arts. Cornelius Agrippa, for example, claimed that the study of magic was the best means to know God and nature. Consequently, Victor himself dabbled in the occult, attempting to raise "ghosts or devils." It isn't surprising then that Victor, once he becomes a student of physiology, fancies himself a modern Prometheus bent on animating lifeless matter, in an effort, he says, to "renew life where death had apparently devoted the body to corruption," presumably so that he can zap his mother back to life. In fact, in his efforts to understand the so-called mystery of life and secrets of heaven, he haunts the graveyards and charnel houses of Ingolstadt, digging up fresh bodies for his own scientific purposes: "I disturbed, with profane fingers, the tremendous secrets of the human frame." What exactly Victor did to the corpses he doesn't say, but he gives us enough detail for us to imagine the rest.

Mary Shelley, just nineteen when she penned the first draft of her seminal Gothic novel Frankenstein, was writing before the scientific revolution of the later 19th century, with its body-snatching industry that supplied medical schools with the freshly dead specimens for their surgical theatres in the stated interest of advancing science and medicine. Her account of Victor's grave-robbing in order to advance science is certainly prescient, especially her foresight of the selfish, prideful motives, and proportionalist justifications.

It's tempting to focus on Victor's obvious character flaws, his defects in logic, and his penchant for playing God, or, for that matter, on the horrifying nature of the monster he creates. What is arguably more enduring and unfortunately lost in the Hollywood perpetuated mythology that has accreted around the 1831 novel is Shelley's trenchant exploration of a perennial question: What does it mean to be human? The genius of Shelley's work lay here as the creature masterfully relates in his own words his auto-didactic education deep in the lonely wilds of a German forest after being rejected by his creator and left for years to his own devices. It is here, after being attacked with stones by local villagers, that Victor's creature takes refuge in a lean-to of a former pigsty at the home of the DeLaceys, a once wealthy French family banished from their home-land for helping a wrongfully accused Muslim merchant escape from a Parisian prison. The living arrangement is an odd but necessary one. The DeLaceys have no idea that this gigantic creature, described by Victor as "a thing such as even Dante could not have conceived," is living in the kennel-like hovel adjacent to their modest cottage. It is from this humble dwelling place carpeted with straw that the creature is able to listen to and observe the family through an imperceptible chink in the wood of their shared wall. Creepy, yes. But this chink serves as a convenient device through which Shelley cleverly allows us to witness the creature's education. It is from this vantage point that he not only learns to read, to speak French, and to under-stand history but witnesses human community, family life, and familial love—and his heart is moved with sympathy as he discovers that people are not naturally hostile, but full of a wide range of emotions, from sadness to joy: "When they were unhappy," he says of the cottagers, "I felt depressed. When they rejoiced, I sympathized in their joys."

The creature also keenly feels the truth that humans need community in order to, well, be fully human. What he is himself, the creature is not yet sure, but his theory is that he is of a new race of man of which he is the lone Adam. "My person was hideous and my stature gigantic," he reflects, when relating his recent history to Victor when they finally meet face-to-face. "What did this mean?"

he asks. "Who was I? What was I? Whence did I come? What was my destination? These questions continually recurred, but I was unable to solve them."

The DeLaceys begin as three: Old Man DeLacey is the paterfamilias. Though blind, he provides stories and music, fatherly love, and moral support for his adult son, Felix, who symbolizes the fruits and pains of human labor, and his teenage daughter, Agatha, who is the embodiment of human beauty. Even in the midst of their family warmth, the creature discovers, the cottagers appear at times to be unhappy. This is partly an effect of their newly begotten state of poverty and banishment. But more importantly, the creature later realizes, much of the family's sadness radiates from Felix's separation from his fiancée, Safie. When months later she arrives on scene after a long travel ordeal from Turkey, the creature marvels at the change that takes place within the family: "I saw that her presence diffused gladness through the cottage, dispelling their sorrow as the sun dissipates the morning mists."

After two years of surreptitiously observing the DeLaceys, the creature believes that, if anyone on earth will sympathize with him, it will be the cottagers. Since the old man is blind, the creature waits until he is alone in his house to make his appeal, to attempt to tell him of his unnatural woes. He knows the old man, without sight, will not recoil in horror and disgust at his ghastly appearance. And although this part of his plan works well, it all goes awry when the others return home to find a monster in their midst. Agatha faints, Safie flees, and Felix chases him away, beating him with a stick. When the creature returns the next day ready to forgive the cottagers, he finds the whole family has moved on, horrified by the prospect of this hideous creature turning up on their doorstep again. The creature's mood turns quickly to rage: He burns the cottage to the ground and leaves for Geneva in search of his creator, vengeance in his heart.

All this is related by the creature to Victor Frankenstein atop a mountain in the Swiss Alps as prelude to making a single request. What does the creature ask of his creator? He wants Victor to do his duty and create for him a helpmate, a female companion with whom he may share his life: "We may not part," he threatens Victor, "until you have promised to comply with my requisition. I am alone and miserable; man will not associate with me; but one as deformed and horrible as myself would not deny herself to me. My companion must be of the same species, and have the same defects. This being you must create."

Through his reading of Milton's *Paradise Lost*—yes, he found a copy of the book and devoured it—the creature knows the story of Adam and Eve, and he's witnessed the light, pleasure, and love that Safie brought into Felix's life. He has seen Felix's transformation and demands of Victor his very own Eve, promising that he'll spirit her away to the wilds of South America to live apart from man in their own Amazonian Garden of Eden.

Though the creature does perhaps garner the sympathy of the reader at times up to this point, Victor remains hard of heart and morally blind. Few will feel his pain, considering that his pride produced this creature, whom he rejected out of fear and cowardice. This same creature goes on to murder Victor's little brother out of vengeance and in an overwrought attempt to attract Victor's attention. So who is responsible for the death of William Frankenstein? This is a question that both Victor and his creature consider. This is a question that astute readers will consider as well. The case can be made that the prideful scientist who disregards both God and natural law in order to serve himself is subject to the law of unintended consequences. Blinded by his pride, Victor is unable or unwilling to recognize that the creature he created is monstrous, his origins unethical and immoral by even the weakest standards. He is also unable to recognize the possible consequences of his bizarre scientific experimentation. Even those who have never read the novel know that Victor Frankenstein is a victim of a monster of his own making—and deservedly so. Victor bears grave responsibility not only for what he himself has done but also for everything the creature does as well—including the string of murders he commits in an effort to make Victor feel as desolated as he has long felt.

No doubt Mary Shelley is prescient when it comes to the misuse of science, whether the Victorian-era body snatchers or 21st-century transhumanists who seek to alter the human person to be more and more like God through the use of genetic engineering, human cloning, IVF, and experimentation with animal human hybrids. Shelley knew even as a teen that human life is not to be manipulated for our own purposes. Victor Frankenstein realizes this too late in the day, only after the monster of his own making has directly or indirectly killed most of Victor's family or friends—and ultimately Victor himself as he considers the havoc that his scientific pride has wreaked on humanity. Pride, after all, is one of the deadliest of sins, and this wasn't lost on Mary Shelley as she penned the first draft of this precursor to the Gothic horror genre of the Victorian age that was to follow.

Above all, it is instructive to note that the novel can be read as a validation of the family, of marriage, and of natural human values in contrast to the overreaching desires of the prideful scientist. The creature struggles to understand who he is, why he was made, where he belongs, and with whom. He considers what it means to be human even as he concludes that he is a singular creature, not created in the image and likeness of God but in the image and likeness of Victor Frankenstein. Too bad that Victor's moral blindness prevents him from becoming fully human himself. Instead he flounders in his own pride to the detriment of his own existence. And the creature? He floats away on an ice raft in the Arctic, vowing to seek rest in death.

"The Body Snatcher" (1884)
ROBERT LOUIS STEVENSON

*B*efore Robert Louis Stevenson became world-renowned for *The Strange Case of Dr. Jekyll and Mr. Hyde,* he wrote a number of short stories delineating many of the themes he would later explore more deeply in his famous novella of 1888. Among these, "The Body Snatcher" is a moral tale of a defective conscience set in the medical world of the late 1820s, one that raises perennial questions about medical ethics, scientific consequentialism, and our general regard for the human body.

Fettes is a fledgling medical student in Stevenson's hometown of Edinburgh. When he receives the attentions of the meteorically famous anatomy professor known only as Mr. K, he believes his life as a successful doctor has been made. In his second year of studies, Fettes is not only handpicked by Mr. K to be "sub assistant" to his classes, he's also offered a side-job to lodge in the same building, adjacent to the dissecting classroom. It is here, after typical nights of mindless carousing, that Fettes "would be called out of bed in the black hours before the winter dawn by the unclean and desperate interlopers who supplied the table." In other words, his primary duty in service to Mr. K was to pay for dead bodies delivered to his door—corpses to be used for dissection in Mr. K's hands-on anatomy course. "In that large and busy class, the raw material of the anatomists kept perpetually running out," which necessitates a steady supply of fresh, new bodies. To Fettes, these nocturnal transactions are simple and routine. He neither feels the need to ask where the bodies come from nor gives much thought to sleeping among the dead. Indeed, Fettes is a young man who is little interested in the fate and fortunes of others, being as he is a slave to his own desires and low ambitions. Like the weak-minded Henry Jekyll of Stevenson's later tale, Fettes manages to function as a respectable and successful gentleman by day but at night indemnifies himself for his nefarious nocturnal duty by "roaring, blackguardly enjoyment" that numbs his conscience. This Scotsman is by all accounts already a confirmed alcoholic.

His employer seems no better. Having served as the moral role model for the younger Fettes, Mr. K's policy is to ask no questions in dealing with the body snatchers (as grave robbers were commonly called). "They bring the body, and we pay the price," says Mr. K, explaining his straightforward *quid pro quo* policy. Though Fettes asks no questions of the abominable Irish ruffians who make their regular deliveries, "he often remarked to himself upon the singular freshness of the bodies." Despite his idle suspicions, he understands his duty to Mr. K includes averting his eyes from any evidence of crime.

One night, however, Fettes recognizes the latest delivered corpse as an acquaintance by the name of Jane Galbraith. "She was alive and hearty yesterday," he protests as he is paying the hang-dog delivery men. "It's impossible she can be dead; it's impossible that you should have got this body fairly," he adds. And that's when it dawns on him that these two men are not grave robbers but cold-blooded murderers, a realization that pricks his otherwise dulled conscience. Knowing that to interfere in this business would be to jeopardize his future medical career and possibly put himself in harm's way, he seeks advice from his immediate superior, a young doctor by the name of Wolfe Macfarlane, "a high favourite among all the reckless students, clever, dissipated, and unscrupulous to the last degree."

It is hardly surprising when Macfarlane, given his lack of moral scrupulosity, counsels Fettes to look the other way. "The fact is," explains the young doctor, "this has been going on too long. Stir up the mud, and you'll get K into the most holy trouble; you'll be in a shocking box yourself." By Macfarlane's reasoning, nothing good will come for him or for Mr. K should Fettes decide to make a moral or legal issue of the matter—and, to be clear, Fettes understands now that Macfarlane is admitting to him that moral and legal issues are at play. "Practically speaking all our subjects have been murdered," Macfarlane admits.

Fettes, who is no moral activist, could have possibly stomached this tough truth had it not been for Jane Galbraith. Here was not just a body, "material" to be cut up and studied by budding medical scientists and future surgeons. Jane was known to him as a real person, someone who had a life to live, with parents and family and friends. Who has the right to take this young woman's life, Fettes wonders, either for personal financial gain or for the universal benefit of science? Fettes's moral life has been jarred and, like a sleeping giant, his conscience is awakening to the horrible reality. Noticing this inconvenient awakening, Macfarlane asks Fettes to consider why Mr. K chose the two of them for his assistants. It wasn't because they were singularly talented. No, explains Macfarlane, it's "because he didn't want old wives." He wanted men who could turn a blind eye to serious crimes. Mr. K was attracted to them because they appeared to him to be bothered little by conscience. They would ask no questions. They would have no qualms about becoming complicit in murder.

A second incident just a few weeks later pricks once again at Fettes's conscience. This time, instead of the Irish rogues, it's Macfarlane at the door in the wee hours with a body in a sackcloth package to deliver for Mr. K's dissecting table. Because Fettes and Macfarlane themselves act in the role of body snatchers from time to time, going out after midnight into the countryside to dig up fresh graves, Fettes is only surprised that Macfarlane went out without him. But once they get the body upstairs and lay it on the table—as routine would have it—Macfarlane tells Fettes he needs to look at the face.

Reluctantly, Fettes uncovers the body to find that he recognizes the face of a Mr. Gray, the man he had dined with the evening before: "The shock was cruel. To see, fixed in the rigidity of death and naked on that coarse layer of sackcloth, the man whom he had left well clad and full of meat and sin upon the threshold of a tavern, awoke, even in the thoughtless Fettes, some of the terrors of the conscience." Macfarlane had introduced him the previous night to this "coarse, vulgar, and stupid man," who appeared to exercise some mysterious control over Macfarlane, as if Gray was threatening blackmail. It had become obvious to Fettes that Macfarlane found Gray to be a "very loathsome rogue." And now, Fettes must grapple with the fact that not only is his closest colleague a murderer but that Macfarlane wants him to become complicit in the crime. "You must pay me," says Macfarlane. "Your accounts, you see, must tally. I dare not give it for nothing, you dare not take it for nothing; it would compromise us both. This is another case like Jane Galbraith's. The more things are wrong the more we must act as if all were right."

Without giving too much thought to the matter, Fettes complies, paying Macfarlane out of Mr. K's cash kept for that sole purpose—just as he would pay the Irish rogues who usually showed up. But to make matters worse, Macfarlane insists on giving Mr. K's money to Fettes. He wants Fettes to "pocket the lucre," not only making him complicit but effectively rendering him helpless to act as a whistleblower. "Suppose I got into trouble, where would you be?" challenges Macfarlane. "This second little matter flows clearly from the first. Mr. Gray is the continuation of Miss Galbraith. You can't begin and then stop. If you begin, you must keep on beginning; that's the truth. No rest for the wicked."

Fettes is at a moral crossroads, and Macfarlane makes clear the choices open to him: He can choose to be either "a lion or a lamb." Offering up a classic false dichotomy, he explains, "If you're a lamb, you'll come to lie upon these tables like Gray or Jane Galbraith; if you're a lion, you'll live and drive a horse like me, like K, like all the world with any wit or courage." The warning is clear: Either Fettes holds his tongue or he will have no prospect of future success, either in the medical profession or elsewise.

Fettes realizes at that this point that he's sinking in a moral quagmire. By taking the blood money, he has fallen from being the arbiter of Macfarlane's destiny to his paid and helpless accomplice. From that point on, Fettes sees no real way out, reasoning that if he didn't have the courage to do the right thing in the past, how could he expect himself to have the courage to do the right thing in the future? His moral weakness and dulled conscience have reduced him to standing idly by to watch students duly dissect the bodies of Jane Galbraith and Mr. Gray and witness their various organs distributed to this table and that for further scientific inspection.

Fettes, like Macfarlane and Mr. K, is a hard man with an ever-hardening heart and a dimming conscience. Three days later he assures Macfarlane that he has "cast in his lot with the lions and forsworn the lambs," confirming that he has fully bought into Mr. K's consequentialist philosophy and his accompanying disregard for the sanctity of the human body. These anatomists were not going to be deterred by the customary piety of burial rights. It was part of their trade "to despise and desecrate the scrolls and trumpets of old tombs, the path worn by the feet of worshippers and mourners and the offerings and inscriptions of bereaved affection." And, as recent history revealed to Fettes, they would not stop at grave robbing and body snatching. They would welcome freshly dead bodies from the most unscrupulous of men, no questions asked. After all, these three men are working in the highly esteemed medical profession, and they reason—pulling a page from Machiavelli's playbook—that the end justifies the means. Ostensibly, they are in this trade in order to advance science and medicine, allowing men and women of future generations to live longer and healthier lives. Or at least, that's what they tell themselves. What is only implied may be closer to the truth: that these anatomists who stand over dead bodies, wielding the burgeoning knowledge about the medical sciences, see themselves as gods among men, suffering under a Promethean delusion.

We have to ask ourselves in our day or any: Is the human body—yes, even the deceased human body—sacred? Or is it merely material to be manipulated by scientists who reason away their desecrations because they are undertaking their experiments or medical procedures in the name of science? Are our internal and external organs merely "stuff" to be harvested, probed, and dissected? These questions soon plague the young Fettes. The next corpse he and Macfarlane disinter from a distant grave bears an uncanny resemblance to Mr. Gray. What Fettes comes to realize after this climactic scene is that he's become a member of an elite sacrificial religion and that he's partaking in its sacred rituals as if he were sacrificing to Baal or Moloch.

Stevenson, writing in the 1880s, dramatized the sordid pursuits of the real-life Dr. Robert Knox, known back in the 1820s as "The Resurrectionist" of the Edinburgh Medical College. Knox is presumably the Mr. K of this tale. In his days, the law allowed only for the bodies of executed criminals to be used by medical schools for the subjects of dissection and study. Because the number of crimes meriting a death sentence fell sharply during that decade, the gap was filled by corpses dug up by grave robbers. (There was no "donating your body to science" in those pre-Victorian days.) Failing that, some of these body snatchers would resort to murder in order to supply bodies for the trade. The Irish rogues of Stevenson's tale are modeled after William Burke and William Hare, who emigrated from Northern Ireland to Scotland to work on the Union Canal project. Between 1827 and 1829, in addition to their grave robberies, the infamous duo suffocated seventeen lodgers, prostitutes, and other unfortunates in and around Edinburgh before they were caught. Although Hare and Knox escaped to England, Burke was brought to justice. After being hanged, his body was publicly dissected at the Edinburgh Medical College, and his skeleton, death mask, and a wallet of his tanned skin were put on public display.

But "The Body Snatcher" is no mere account of 1820s Scotland. Its timelessness can be found in its exploration of medical ethics, scientism, and a scientific consequentialism that claims the "end" of medical experimentation (the advancement of science) justifies the "means" (using the human body and its parts as utilitarian "stuff"). With today's hot-button biotech issues, who can deny that themes of "The Body Snatcher" are relevant today? Yes, these may be expressed in different ways during the 21st century, but moral and ethical issues involving scientific research and medical experimentation are as relevant as ever—arguably more so! Consider, for example, embryonic stem cell research in which the embryo is destroyed in the process of extracting its stem cells. Destroying embryos for the purpose of harvesting their parts reduces nascent human life to the moral status of mold. Or consider abortion. As if the willful taking of human life isn't morally bad enough, not to mention evil, some medical research companies have purchased aborted babies to harvest their parts. To give one example of many: In 2017, two of Planned Parenthood's business partners, DaVinci Biosciences and DV Biologics, admitted to selling aborted baby body parts from Planned Parenthood. Just a few years earlier, in 2012, Planned Parenthood charged a biospecimen company nearly $25,000 for "fetal tissue" and maternal blood samples. Further, some of the vaccines currently used to prevent diseases such as rubella, measles, rabies, polio, hepatitis A, and chickenpox are produced using fetal embryo fibroblast cells from human abortions. In all of these 21st-century cases, human body parts are treated as commodities to be bought and sold, all in the name of medical progress, much the same as in Mr. K's time.

Because of their experience with Mr. Gray's doppel-ganger corpse, Macfarlane and Fettes eventually go their separate ways. Macfarlane, the consummate lion, becomes a rich and successful London doctor, while Fettes, who has apparently disavowed the questionable ethics of the medical establishment, languishes as an out-at-the-elbows small-town drunk, decades later still struggling to drown the horrors he witnessed and endured in pursuit of respectability and fame in the highly lucrative medical profession. Despite Macfarlane's worldly success, there's something in the telling of Stevenson's tale to suggest that it is Macfarlane—not Fettes—who will come to a truly bad end. Even though Fettes, with his "crapulous, disreputable vices," enjoys no success and is drinking away his days in the local pub, we can see even his weak conscience has provided a path to his own eventual redemption.

Never Let Me Go (2005)

KAZUO ISHIGURO

*K*azuo Ishiguro's *Never Let Me Go* does not read like the typical dystopian novel as it is often labelled because it really isn't one. It's a beautifully atmospheric love story—we even get a classic love triangle—about real human beings who turn out to be clones bred as property of the British government's "donation programme." The clones' ultimate purpose in life is to serve others by donating their vital organs, one at a time, until they "complete," the euphemism here for eventually dying of complications due to live organ donation. The most fortunate among them live to complete their fourth donation, but most seem to die after a second or third. The important fact that Ishiguro's main characters are all clones comes as a surprise well into the novel, not only to the unsuspecting reader but also to Kathy, Tommy, and Ruth, three students educated from infancy at Hailsham, an exclusive boarding school secluded in the bucolic English countryside.

The story, told by an adult Kathy, is a reflection on their discovery of the reason, meaning, and purpose of their lives as "donors," as they are called. As the narrative unfolds, it becomes apparent that none of the Hailsham students has parents or siblings or anything resembling family. Their student years seem an unlikely hybrid of a co-ed Eton and a state-sponsored group home. Though Ishiguro makes the case through his narrative that these

clones are as human as anyone—they love, they back-
bite, they create artwork and even write poetry—they
are denied their basic human rights, forced into a utilitarian existence, ultimately seen and used as a collection
of body parts to be harvested for the good of privileged
others. In many ways, it would be accurate to compare
the Hailsham students to sheep being led to the slaughter.
What's truly ingenious about this novel is that the world
Ishiguro describes is not some far-flung future driven
by technology still on the distant horizon. It is our own
world—or at least recognizable as Britain in the 1980s
and 90s, a time of the Walkman and cassette tapes rather
than smart phones and Netflix.

Madame Marie-Claude, a seemingly stern French over-
seer visits Hailsham two or three times each year to choose
the best of the student artwork for her rumored "Gallery."
Though Kathy and the others are never able to confirm
the existence of an actual art gallery, the fact remains that
it is "a most distinguished honour" to have work selected
by Madame for whatever her true purpose might be. It
is that purpose that is the subject of great consterna-
tion through the years. When a student one day breaks
an unwritten rule and asks one of their guardians why
Madame "takes our things away," all she can say is that
"it's for a good reason. A very important reason." Though
she's not prepared to tell the students this good reason,
she says she hopes that one day it'll be explained to them.

During Madame's impersonal visits, the students notice
that she studiously avoids them and even wonders if she
fears them. During one visit, Ruth convinces six other
students to test the hypothesis. When Madame arrives
they all approach her at once. "It wasn't as though Madame
did anything other than what we predicted she'd do: she
just froze and waited for us to pass. She didn't shriek, or
even gasp," reflects Kathy years later, but "I can still see it
now, the shudder she seemed to be suppressing, the real

dread that one of us would accidentally brush against her." Ruth had been right: Madame *was* afraid of the Hailsham students, but "in the same way someone might be afraid of spiders," she explains. It had never occurred to them how they might feel being seen as the equivalent of creepy eight-legged creatures.

Kathy later reflects on that encounter, now as an adult understanding its significance: This was the moment she realized that the Hailsham students were somehow essentially different from others, "that there are people out there, like Madame, who don't hate you or wish you harm, but who nevertheless shutter at the very thought of you—of how you were brought into this world and why—and who dread the idea of your hand brushing against theirs."

Along the way to the big reveal, Ishiguro drops other hints that things are not as they seem at happy Hailsham. He is able to do it so subtly that we take little notice at the clues when they first tumble to us. Rumors, for example, circulate about what has happened to students who had "run off beyond the Hailsham boundaries" into the woods. One boy was found two days later tied to a tree with his feet and hands cut off. And another climbed over the fence just to see what it was like outside, got lost, and died: "Her ghost was always wandering about the woods, gazing over Hailsham, pining to be let back in."

And then there were the draconian restrictions about smoking. Not only were students not permitted to smoke, the guardians, Kathy explains, "made sure to give us some lecture any time any references to cigarettes came along. Even if we were shown a picture of a famous writer or world leader, and they happened to have a cigarette in their hand, then the lesson would grind to a halt." And that was in addition to the actual lessons directly inculcating the evils of smoking, showing them "horrible pictures of what smoking did to the insides of your body." This was especially important for Hailsham students, they were told, since they were "special."

These hints of foreshadowing, of course, are not at all removed from the world we know. Rumors of strange happenings in the woods, adults that recoil at students as if they were spiders, and overkill lectures on the perils of smoking are hardly beyond the pale in the life of even the 21st-century boarding school. Yet once Kathy and her friends discover the real truth about themselves, it all resonates for them as it does for the reader. Those stories about the ghastly happenings in the woods served to instill fear, working as effectively as a tall barbed-wire fence in keeping them willingly impounded on their beautiful campus. Those lectures on smoking that bordered on indoctrination sessions thwarted an addiction that could have compromised lungs and kidneys and heart that would eventually require harvesting in their capacity as donors.

As the students progress through their education they increasingly become self-aware—first of their purpose in life as "donors," then that they are, unlike others in the "outside world," incapable of having children. And finally, that they are human clones, regarded by others as no more than bio-material owned by an unseen government program that dictates the trajectory of their lives. At times, when the students would imagine themselves growing up to be famous actors or working in a beautiful office building or delivering the mail for the Royal Post, someone—either guardian or fellow student—would bring them back to reality, reviving the undercurrent of hopelessness. In one scene, Miss Lucy, the only guardian who even hints that she objects to the donation program, breaks down with some straight talk. She tells the students that "none of you will be film stars. And none of you will be working at supermarkets as I heard some of you planning the other day. Your lives are set out for you. You'll become adults, then before you're old, before

you're even middle-aged, you'll start to donate your vital
organs. That's what each of you was created to do....
You were brought into this world for a purpose, and your
futures, all of them, have been decided." Miss Lucy also
explains that before they begin donating, they will serve
for a time as "carer," assisting donors as they navigate
the donation process—operations, post-op recovery, and
eventual death. In the early years of having this knowledge,
around age 13, the students imagine that when their time
comes, they'll just unzip a bit of themselves, "a kidney
or something would slide out, and you'd hand it over,"
says Kathy. A few years later, when the reality becomes
more apparent to them, they simply avoid bringing up
the subject altogether. It is too somber, too depressing,
to be actively contemplated.

One important part of their Hailsham education is
discovering in sex ed class that none of the donor students, male or female, could have babies. Because of this
infertility and the understanding that their sole purpose
in life is to donate their vital organs so that others may
live longer, healthier lives, the Hailsham headmistress
Miss Emily gives "a lot of sex lectures" demonstrating
with human skeletons exactly how it is done: "She was
going through all the nuts and bolts of how you did it,
what went in where, the different variations, like this was
still Geography." Since the procreative aspect of sex didn't
come into play, the point of Miss Emily's lecturing—like
many 21st-century sex ed lectures—is to fully eliminate
the unitive aspect of sex, instead treating the whole subject
like a mechanical function of the body similar to urina-
tion. No emotion, no love. The upshot: It really doesn't
matter who does it with whom. Sex is introduced as just
one among many pleasures, like reading or watching television programs. Of course, as you might guess, it turns
out that sex isn't actually that simple or mechanical in
reality. Emotions do come into play, creating jealousies

and sometimes irreconcilable misunderstandings. And the times they do not, it's easy to see that the Hailsham students are being taught to regard each other as donors at best and playthings to be used and abused at worst. One student had a theory "that it was [the Hailsham guardians'] duty to make us have sex because otherwise we wouldn't be good donors later on.... Things like your kidneys and pancreas didn't work properly unless you kept having sex."

Once graduated from Hailsham at age 16, the students are sent to assigned group living arrangements with "donor" students from other government-run boarding schools, which turn out to be less blessed with amenities than those provided at Hailsham. Kathy, Tommy, and Ruth all end up at a refurbished farmstead called The Cottages, where they wile away two years reading classic novels and having "inconsequential sex" with one another before heading out to mysterious "courses," which they figure out quickly enough have something to do with becoming carers. The Hailsham three watch as the veteran students, one after the next, quietly leave The Cottages. Their departure, Kathy notes, is followed by a strict taboo of "taking care not to mention them," since they all know that's what their short-term fate looks like too.

It is here where Ruth is confronted by Chrissie and Rodney, a non-Hailsham couple who wants to know the details of a rumor—*a Hailsham rumor* that more or less guides the second half of the novel and leads years later to Kathy and Tommy's discovery of the truth about themselves. Chrissie explains that they've heard that some Hailsham students in the past, in special circumstances, had managed to get a deferral for three to four years from becoming a donor. "What they said," Chrissie explains, "was that if you are a boy and a girl, and you were in love with each other, really properly in love, and you could show it, then the people who run Hailsham, they sorted it out for you." This is news to Kathy, Tommy, and Ruth. They've never heard of such a rumor, but through the years, it gets them all to thinking.

Tommy has a theory that Madame's gallery is somehow connected to the love deferral, that the artwork selected to be taken away from Hailsham students could later be used as evidence to prove that a couple is truly in love. Miss Emily, Tommy explains, once told them that "things like pictures, poetry, and all that kind of stuff, they revealed what you were like inside. She said they revealed your soul." And, he reasons, this must be the way to judge if a boy and a girl, a man and a woman, are truly in love. It's revealed through artwork and poetry. "The point is," he says, "whoever decides, Madame or whoever it is, they need something to go on."

Although Tommy's theory doesn't pan out, he has inadvertently tapped into an important truth, not only that art and poetry does indeed reflect one's soul, but that they—the clone donors—*actually have a soul*, no different from everyone else. Little does he know at the time, but that assumption is a controversial one throughout Ishiguro's Britain. In fact, Kathy and Tommy don't find this out until at least a decade later, after Ruth has "completed" following her third donation and Tommy is getting ready for his fourth. At Ruth's earlier suggestion, Tommy and Kathy seek out Madame in order to "apply" for a deferral, having convinced themselves that they are indeed truly in love. And they believe they have the artwork to prove it.

By this time, Hailsham has been closed for some years, though it is not clear to Kathy and Tommy why. When they arrive at Madame's home in a distant city, Kathy observes, "I don't know if she recognized us at that point; but without a doubt she saw and decided in a second *what we were,* because you could see her stiffen—as if a pair of large spiders was set to crawl toward her." Ironically, Madame turns out to be perhaps the most sympathetic to the clones and their hopeless plight, tearing up during their conversation. "Poor creatures," she says. "What did we do to you? With all our schemes and plans?" No, she tells them, there is not and never was any deferral for love. And no, her "gallery" has nothing to do with this deferral rumor. Conveniently, Hailsham's old headmistress, Miss Emily, lives in the same house. It is she who provides the explanations. "We took away your art," she admits, "because we thought it would reveal your souls. Or to put it more finely, we did it to prove you had souls at all." The idea that clones were like normal human beings was not widely accepted, and yes, there was some question as to whether a creature modelled from the DNA of a naturally born human would even possess a soul. Hailsham, Miss Emily clarifies, was actually established to challenge the way that the government's "donations programme" was run. Clones, she says, were raised in deplorable conditions that, for Hailsham students, are "hardly imaginable." Miss Emily and Madame both believed that these clones should be treated as the humans they are. "We demonstrated to the world that if students were reared in humane, cultivated environments, it was possible for them to grow to be as sensitive and intelligent as any ordinary human being. Before that," says Miss Emily, "all clones—or *students*, as we preferred to call you—existed only to supply medical science."

Ishiguro is digging into medical ethics debates of the early 21st century by exploring them in a dramatized alternative Britain of the late 20th century. The questions posed by the novel are the same important questions posed by medical ethics today. The primary question from which all others derive is a familiar one: What does it mean to be human? As we begin to use advanced medical technologies to produce or enhance human life, Ishiguro suggests, we must keep in mind that all human beings have their accompanying rights, duties, and responsibilities. We cannot play God, as does Ishiguro's government through its inhumane "donations program," which has created a shadow race of second-class citizens, treated essentially as property rather than as human beings with dignity and inviolable rights. Further, Ishiguro also suggests that we cannot take advantage of those in desperate circumstances, as we do in our own society through fertility services which harvest women's eggs and men's sperm or, say, as the Chinese Communist Party does by harvesting organs from live political prisoners, especially members of the Falun Gong religious group—a horrific ongoing human rights abuse to which the rest of the world continues to turn a blind eye.

It is this denial of the right to exercise free will that pervades the whole of *Never Let Me Go,* so much so, so thoroughly, that it never even dawns on any of the clones that they needn't seek a deferral from another human being, but that they could branch out on their own and pursue their own lives, marry, adopt children, have a career, and contribute to society in one of an infinite number of ways. Ishiguro conspicuously leaves out any mention of God as creator. Any recognition that human beings are created in the image and likeness of God would provide the philosophical foundation to overthrow the government's inhumane donations program. That's precisely why Miss Emily and Madame are helpless in the end, despite their best intentions with Hailsham, treating the clones like the humans they are. "It might look like you were simply pawns in a game," Miss Emily explains to Kathy and Tommy. "It can certainly be looked at like that. But think of it. You were lucky pawns."

The Constant Gardener (2001)
JOHN LE CARRÉ

*B*eautiful, wealthy, and well-educated Tessa Quayle is a kind of young and flirtatious Mother Theresa with a big heart for the poorest of the world. She is also a whistleblower who has witnessed a monstrous injustice and has gone out to fight it with a quixotic zeal that gets her brutally murdered in the opening pages of *The Constant Gardener*, John le Carré's morality tale about the profiteering of pharmaceutical companies that use poor and desperate black Africans as guinea pigs for their clinical trials. "Tessa was murdered to keep her quiet," says one insider in her testimony to police. "Anyone who takes on the pharmaceutical industry is liable to get her throat cut. Some pharmaceutical companies are arms dealers in shining raiment."

Africa, Tess discovers in the years leading up to her death, is "the pharma dustbin of the world," and white self-styled humanitarians are ripping off the poorest nations. "Every time I hear a pharma justifying its actions on the grounds of Humanity, Altruism, Duty to Mankind, I want to vomit," says Tess. The multi-billion-dollar pharmaceutical industry is, instead, inspired by what another character aptly calls "the god Profit." It's not about offering charitable, humanitarian relief to those most in need, says Tessa; it's "an irresponsible quest for corporate profit" using the cover of what the world often calls humanitarianism. It sacrifices the poor of Africa for the so-called "greater good" of the American and European markets, where billions stand to be reaped.

Justin Quayle, the widower whom Tessa leaves behind, is a mid-level foreign service officer at the British High Commission in Nairobi, Kenya, where Tessa kept busy helping the poor and needy and where her crusade against big pharma was carried out unbeknownst to her husband, an absurdly happy skeptic in a straw hat, who weeds and prunes his way through flower beds, worried about keeping them sandy enough to grow his yellow freesias. But Justin's studied ignorance soon transforms into moral purpose. The novel chronicles Justin's quest through England, Italy, Canada, Sudan, and back to Kenya, to unmask his wife's murderers. In the process, he takes up Tessa's cause to expose the amoral Swiss-Canadian pharmaceutical giant Karel Vita Hudson (KVH) and ThreeBees, its distributor in Africa. In doing so, he falls afoul of the British Foreign Office, who it turns out has been complicit all along. In response to his rogue investigation, Justin's former colleagues accuse him of chasing conspiracy theories. "If you can't deal with reality," says his former boss Sandy Woodrow, "then dream up a conspiracy. What precise conspiracy Justin has dreamed up—and where *we* come into it, we in the High Commission—whether we're in league with the freemasons, or the Jesuits, or the Ku Klux Klan, or the World Bank—I'm afraid I can't enlighten you." Woodrow, of course, is concerned that Justin has hit the "conspiracy trail" because Woodrow himself is part of the problem, and the best way to discredit a man who risks exposing you is to consign him to the rank of conspiracy theorist. During Woodrow's interview with Scotland Yard after Tessa's death, one insightful investigator turns to him and says, "People like you should be stopped. You think you're solving the world's problems but actually you're the problem."

Justin discovers that, at the time of her death, Tessa was investigating the new anti-tuberculosis drug Dypraxa, manufactured by KVH and distributed throughout Africa by ThreeBees. The blight of tuberculosis lately resurfaced in Africa as an HIV-related plague resistant to traditional medications and predictions, and, as Justin discovers from the notes and research Tessa left behind, the richest nations will soon be facing a tubercular pandemic, and Dypraxa will become the multi-billion-dollar earner that all good shareholders dream of. "If the TB market performs as forecast," Tessa wrote in notes she left behind, "billions and billions of dollars are waiting to be earned, and the boy to earn them is Dypraxa—always provided, of course, that the preliminary canter over the course in Africa has not thrown up any disturbing side effects."

And this is the very conflict at hand: Tessa and others have discovered that the experimental use of Dypraxa throughout the poorest African nations has indeed thrown up disturbing side effects. In fact, Tessa has witnessed women being poisoned by the drug in the slums around Nairobi. She has proof that KVH is using sick Africans as guinea pigs to determine the side effects, reasoning that many of these poor and destitute will die anyway, so why not experiment on them with this fledgling wonder drug? This is the kind of rationalization that disturbs Tessa and her pharma watchdog colleagues. They witness Dypraxa being used in Kenya before the results are in from legitimate clinical trials. One of the honchos at ThreeBees even admits that "every patient is in some degree a test case for the benefit of the greater good," which is presumably the First World market. This, Tessa points out, is unethical and immoral, especially considering that the negative results of clinical trials are being systematically covered up by the pharmaceutical giant and its acolytes.

In his pursuit of justice for Tessa, Justin discovers all her notes and contacts that confirm the ongoing cover-up of the unethical scientific methods being used in the name of big business. This leads him to Dr. Lara Emrich, one of the co-discovers of the molecule used to make Dyp-raxa. When he finds her down-and-out in Saskatchewan, she explains to Justin that KVH provided her dedicated research laboratories, a team of technicians, clinical trials all over the Third World, first class travel, glamorous hotels, respect and money galore. After two years, however, Emrich made an unfortunate discovery: The KVH trials were fraudulent. They had not been scientifically written but were designed only to get the drug onto the market as soon as possible. Serious side effects were deliberately excluded. Emrich, like Tessa, was a whistleblower, prepared to "out" the pharma giant for its unethical modus operandi. Her three primary claims were that 1) the side effects are being deliberately concealed in the interest of profits, 2) the world's poorest communities are being used as guinea pigs by the world's richest, and 3) legitimate scientific debate of these issues is stifled by corporate intimidation.

All the while, the KVH clinical trials were being reported favorably in important medical journals by dis-tinguished opinion leaders who failed to declare their profitable connections with KVH. But when Emrich tried to publish an article in a medical journal concerning her own conclusions, KVH sued the journal, stopped distri-bution of the article, sacked Emrich, and destroyed her reputation and career. "Speak out," she tells Justin, and "they take away your salary, fire you, and run you out of town. Free speech comes mighty costly."

Tessa had discovered a pattern. Anyone who presents any argument in the medical journals against Dypraxa is ridiculed and dismissed as irresponsible—or worse. "Big pharmas spend zillions buying up scientists and medics to plug their product," wrote Tessa. "Unbought scientific opinion is increasingly hard to find." Articles, she found, are routinely planted by KVH in even the so-called qual-ity journals like *The Lancet* and the *New England Journal of Medicine*. And these influential journals are presumed to present new medical facts which are not to be disputed. Tessa called this "faith in the clinical gospels," the tendency for students and clinicians to treat this pharma-bought literature with undue respect.

At one point in his investigation, Justin asks Dr. Emrich why so few people complain or object to KVH's unethical approach to its clinical trials. Third World doctors, medical workers, the distributor, the local health authorities—none of these wish to lose the enormous profits from the whole range of KVH drugs. The financial stakes are too high to act ethically or to be honest. Money has clouded their moral judgment. And the patients—most of them hail from undemocratic countries with corrupt politicians and officials who pocket huge bribes. "The victims," she says, "are the man on the street, the uprooted, the poor and the very poor. And the children who will have no future."

If *The Constant Gardener* is a cautionary tale, it is one that warns of a medical profession compromised by the pharmaceutical companies turning their backs on God. "The modern pharmaceutical industry is only sixty-five years old," explains one of Tessa's watchdog colleagues. "It has good men and women, it has achieved human and social miracles, but its collective conscience is not developed." Many of the self-styled humanitarians involved in the distribution of Dypraxa in Africa, she says, claim that they love God and the whole world, but they also love hard currency and the "god Profit." Yes, they believe in God, but they ignore Him. They have instead set up an idol to which they sacrifice the poorest and most destitute.

Perhaps it is no coincidence that Tessa is a Roman Catholic who not only believes in God but loves people— not "humanity" but individual persons, especially those most in need. It is convenient perhaps that she's been left with a sizable inheritance and is thus wholly impervious to the temptations of financial gain, enabling her to more easily pursue truth and justice at any expense. Throughout the novel, flashbacks provide us with a portrait of a young woman who, far from perfect, is dedicated to carrying out the corporal works of mercy in a very personal way, involving herself in the lives of the indigenous poor, even at her own expense. Justin, who obviously adored Tessa in their brief married years, discovers through his quest that his wife was a woman of incredible fortitude, operating out of love and virtue—a realization that changes his own outlook toward his former profession and toward the world. Unlike Tessa, Justin has never believed in God. But late in his quest he realizes that he's treated the British Foreign Office as an idol. He has served it as his God. "There was a time when I believed it was expedient that one man—or woman—should die for the benefit of many," he reflects. "I called it sacrifice, or duty, or necessity. There was a time when I could stand outside the Foreign Office at night and stare up at its lighted windows and think: Good evening, it's your humble servant, Justin. I'm a piece of the great wise engine, and proud of it." Although in the end he repudiates this idol, it isn't clear if Tessa's belief in the one true God has penetrated his secular Englishman's armor.

It's worth noting that Le Carré includes an afterword "author's note" in which he takes great pains to disclaim that no entity in his novel—not the British High Commission in Nairobi, not KVH, not Three Bees, or any of the characters—resembles any real institution or person. "But I can tell you this," he writes, punctuating his disclaimer. "As my journey through the pharmaceutical jungle progressed, I came to realize that, by comparison with reality, my story was as tame as a holiday postcard."

One important question to ask, presented by the fiction of *The Constant Gardener*, is this: Does the international pharmaceutical industry indeed use destitute black Africans as guinea pigs for its clinical trials? Consider that in 2020, when the rush was on to come up with a vaccine for COVID-19, viral perpetrator of pandemic, the first large-scale clinical trials were set up in Cameroon, Uganda, Tanzania, Kenya, and in the poorest parts of South Africa. For some reason, the World Health Organization (WHO) deemed that Africa was most in need of being vaccinated. Those clinical trials—as in Le Carré's novel—are being carried out on the poorest black Africans. No sane person would argue that Africans are not as deserving as those on any other continent of receiving a vaccine to a potentially deadly disease. But that's not what's in question here. WHO, along with self-styled humanitarians, framed the trials as a humanitarian gesture to "those most in need." Do not be fooled: Black Africans of the poorest nations are being used as guinea pigs for this vaccine, a vaccine which anyone in the scientific community can tell you is not yet ready for human distribution. This is just one of a number of examples that could be offered of Big Pharma "humanitarianism." John le Carré predicted this two decades ago, and one wonders how long Africa will be treated as the Big Pharma playground.

"*Markheim*" (1885)

ROBERT LOUIS STEVENSON

*A*fter committing murder for the first time, Markheim, the protagonist in the eponymous short story by Robert Louis Stevenson, is confronted at the scene of his crime by a mysterious "visitant" who seems to be giving him advice on how best to escape being caught. Markheim, a former petty thief, has killed an antique dealer in cold blood on Christmas day in order to have time to steal the shopkeeper's money, which he knows to be hidden away somewhere in the building. His singular objective is to find the money before the shopkeeper's maidservant returns and discovers her master dead in a pool of his own blood. In the midst of his search, the visitant, whom Markheim describes as "neither of earth nor of God," suddenly appears—not to accuse but seemingly to abet. The mysterious visitor even advises Markheim to kill the maidservant upon her return, removing the only obstacle from his plan to steal the shopkeeper's loot. Although Markheim clearly believes this mysterious visitor is the devil—after all, he seems to be tempting Markheim to commit further mortal sins—the visitant is actually his guardian angel, using a kind of reverse psychology in order to set Markheim on an unlikely path to redemption.

Stevenson, who famously explored the concept of the human conscience in the face of evil in his novella *Dr. Jekyll and Mr. Hyde,* uses "Markheim" to provide a concise dramatization of the power of repentance. No sin is too great for God to forgive. Although the entire story takes place within the span of an hour, Markheim undergoes a remarkable transformation during this brief time: He walks into the antique shop a calculating criminal and leaves a repentant sinner. A gambler by vice, the London lowlife has brought 36 years' worth of sins with him into the shop on this Christmas day; even before he commits the murder, his conscience is already busy accusing him. When Markheim claims he's looking to buy his fiancée a Christmas gift, the dealer suggests a 15th-century hand-held mirror. "I ask you for a Christmas present, and you give me this," Markheim snaps at the dealer, "—this damned reminder of years, and sins and follies—this hand conscience!" Clearly, he is not fond of seeing his own reflection. To him, a mirror is not just a mirror but an unwelcome invitation to reflect on a squandered and dissolute life.

As soon as Markheim stabs the dealer with a long, skewer-like dagger, he realizes the entire shop is filled with antique mirrors in which he sees "an army of spies" watching him, accusing him. To add to the mood, all the clocks in the showroom chime together the hour of three in the afternoon (the hour of agony), reminding Markheim that he has but limited time to carry out his task: to find the money and leave the shop before the maidservant returns. But the clocks and the mirrors become auditory and visual catalysts for his conscience, which quickly kicks in. "In many rich mirrors ... he saw his face repeated and repeated, as it were an army of spies; his own eyes met and detected him." At this point his conscience is merely worrying him: He second-guesses his planning of the mortal deed, faulting himself for not choosing a "quieter hour" or preparing an alibi. He questions his use of a knife as the fatal weapon and his overall lack of caution. He should have done things otherwise, he obsesses. His fear is simple; he worries he'll be caught, arrested, tried, convicted, and hanged. In short, he fears the law.

Curiously, although he fears the justice of man, about God himself Markheim is at ease; he rationalizes his savage act, believing that God will understand his extenuating circumstances, that he is "a bond slave to poverty," that he was driven by desperation. In sum, Markheim is presuming God's mercy will excuse him and perhaps forgive him—without the necessity of further movement of his own heart.

It is ironic then that it is his fear of the law that stirs his conscience, sets his mind racing, playing tricks on him: "Brute terrors like the scurrying of rats in a deserted attic, filled the more remote chambers of his brain with riot." He sees in his mind's eye the arrest, the trial, the prison, the gallows, and the black coffin. He imagines the eyes of the holiday revelers outside the house penetrating the brick walls and shuttered windows of the antique shop, pointing at him accusingly, crying out to all of London that he, Markheim, is a murderer. Worst of all, he begins to hear little noises throughout the house—"the stir of delicate footing" and other barely perceptible sounds that make him conscious of some presence.

Although, intellectually, he knows no one is in the house but him, he hears footsteps on the stairs, echoing his own, as he climbs to the second-floor offices. In other words, he hears the echo of his own footsteps and fears not being alone. The fear grows by the minute: "The sense that he was not alone grew upon him to the verge of madness." Once Markheim reaches the second floor and enters the shop keeper's office, he is terrorized by the sound of steps coming up the stairs after him. "A step mounted the stair, slowly and steadily, and presently a hand was laid upon the knob, and the lock clicked, and the door opened." Oddly enough, a man opens the door to the office, pops his head into the room, nods, and turns around to—seemingly—head back downstairs.

This is too much for Markheim. He lets out a scream, and the visitor returns, asking calmly, almost comically,

"Did you call me?" To make matters worse, Markheim notices that the visitant looks eerily like himself: a doppelganger! This perhaps marks the beginning of Markheim's change of heart. The visitant claims he can tell Markheim where to find the money and warns him that the maidservant is presently on her way and will return in a matter of minutes. Markheim must make his move quickly, and the visitant offers his assistance. But his advice is brutal: wait for the maidservant, he tells Markheim, and then invite her in and kill her too. This will assure Markheim enough time to loot the whole place. But the visitant follows up this advice with the cool assertion that even if Markheim steals the money, he'll lose it quickly on the stock market, just as he has done time and time again. In fact, adds the visitant, Markheim will continue his moral descent: "You will never change." No wonder Markheim believes this visitant is a devil come to mock him and accuse him. The more the two converse, the more Markheim believes he's speaking with the devil himself until eventually, he begins to reject the advice he's being given. He believes he's finally come face to face with evil, face to face with the devil himself—and in the face of true evil, Markheim is afraid. "I begin to see myself all changed," he tells the visitant, assuring him that this devil (as he sees him) will surely lay no claim to him.

And so begins Markheim's transformation from morally destitute murderer to repentant sinner, throwing himself on the mercy of God. The maidservant has now arrived. Markheim must make his move. The visitant reiterates what needs to be done: He must kill again if he wishes to escape the law. Fortunately, Markheim sees another path open up to him. He must confess, turn himself in, and give himself up to the justice of man in order to receive God's mercy. "I can cease from action," he says. "If my life be an ill thing, I can lay it down." And, curiously, once Markheim makes the decision to turn himself in, the visitant's features also make a remarkable transformation, "a wonderful and lovely change; they brightened and softened with a tender triumph, and even as they brightened, faded, and dislimned," reflecting perhaps what's in Markheim's heart: a kind of true conversion, even if built on the foundation of imperfect contrition. Yes, he reasons, it is better to give myself up to the justice of men if it means I have a chance of thwarting the life of everlasting hell that the devil has prepared for me.

And so, in a twist on the idea of a deathbed conversion, Markheim tells the maidservant as he opens the door to her, "You had better go for the police. I have killed your master."

The Tragical History of Doctor Faustus (c. 1592)

CHRISTOPHER MARLOWE

William Shakespeare is, without a doubt, the greatest of Elizabethan playwrights. And many scholars agree that Shakespeare is the most accomplished dramatist the world has ever seen. But before Shakespeare came onto the scene, Christopher Marlowe was the leading light of Elizabethan London, and, like Shakespeare, Marlowe was cloaked in mystery. In fact, he was the subject of a number of contradictory accusations during his short professional life: He was at once accused of being an atheist and of being a Catholic, the latter a sometimes capital offense during the reign of Elizabeth Tudor. Marlowe was also accused of being a spy for the Catholics even as he was accused of infiltrating the Catholic community as a spy for the queen. All we really know is that he left the University of Cambridge under a cloud of suspicion and died a few years later in a knife pub brawl at the hands of men known to work for the queen. His untimely death came at the age of 29.

That didn't leave Christopher Marlowe much time to give the world his literary genius. He wrote just five plays. His most enduring work: *The Tragical History of Doctor Faustus*.

Set in early-16th-century Wittenberg, Germany, home to Martin Luther's Protestant revolt, the play was based off the bizarre, legendary accounts of occultist Johannes

Faustus. The Dr. Faustus of Marlowe's play is a prideful professor whose moral judgment and rational intellect become clouded by his desire to, essentially, be like God. But instead of imitating Christ, Faustus rejects logic, medicine, law, philosophy, and theology—every branch of medieval learning—as "odious and obscure" meant only for "petty wits."

Searching for knowledge more profound, he enlists the aid of Cornelius and Valdes, two well-known astrologers, to initiate him into the dark arts. Faustus's life as a necromancer begins by racking the name of Christ, abjuring the scriptures, and conjuring Mephostophilis, a helper devil whom he finds so hideous that he asks the demon to go back to Hell and return to him in the form of an elderly Franciscan friar—the form, he says, that suits a devil best.

And here's where we get the eponymous concept of the Faustian bargain. Dr. Faustus asks to make a deal with the devil, using Mephostophilis as his intermediary. The Faustian bargain, as a trope used in literature, has three essential parts: 1) a deal is struck through a contract, handshake, or some other formal agreement; 2) the deal involves a short-term gain; this can be money, worldly influence, authority, supernatural powers, you name it; and 3) the bargain results in a long term loss. In the original Faustian bargain, Dr. Faustus sells his eternal soul (the long-term loss) for 24 years of having Mephostophilis as his servant, granting his every desire (the short-term gain). He seals the deal by signing a contract with his own blood.

But not without some warning. Three warnings, in fact. The first comes from his faculty colleagues, the so-called "scholars of Wittenburg," who all fawn over Faustus's gargantuan intellect. The irony is that his colleagues, who represent rational human nature, are petty wits compared to Faustus, yet it is they who see the blatant folly of dabbling in necromancy. Faustus, on the other hand, is spiritually, morally, and intellectually blind by this time in his career. The second warning comes from a character simply called the "Good Angel," often interpreted as the well-formed bit of Dr. Faustus's conscience. The Good Angel fittingly has an evil counterpart—the so-called Bad Angel, who you might say represents temptation. Good Angel on the right shoulder. Bad Angel on the left. Thus begins the ongoing battle for the soul of Dr. Faustus, a concept known in literature as *psychomachia*. Dr. Faustus's third warning comes from an unlikely source: Mephostophilis himself, who testifies that being deprived of the everlasting bliss of Heaven is like ten thousand hells. "O Faustus," implores the devil's minion, "leave these frivolous demands / which strike a terror to my fainting soul."

Another irony creeps forth here, made possible only by the brilliant scholar's clouded spiritual and moral judgment: Dr. Faustus misinterprets Mephostophilis's explanation of Hell, seeing it merely as a separation from God, which Faustus says he's already enjoying in his celebrated life here on earth. In fact, he says he scorns those "joys" he will never possess, for who needs to be in the presence of God, if someone such as himself can simply go on, endlessly. But Faustus marches on, claiming that Hell and its torments are mere wives' tales, despite the fact that he recently summoned a demon so hideous that he ordered him to return to Hell and come back to him in the innocuous form of an elderly friar.

Though Faustus ultimately heeds not these three warnings, he is troubled by conscience when it comes to signing his soul away. With pen in hand, dipped in his own blood, the words "*Homo fuge!*" (fly, man!) appear on his arm and the blood on his pen congeals—a clear divine intervention if there ever was one. "What might the staying of my blood portend?" Faustus lamely considers. "Whither should I fly?" he wonders. But Faustus convinces himself he has nowhere to run but to God who, he says, will fling him to Hell for his sins. With Mephostophilis assisting with a candle flame to melt the doctor's congealed blood, Faustus signs away his soul for 24 years of earthly pleasures.

You'd think 24 years is plenty of time to enjoy the best the world has to offer. Faustus, in fact, has grand plans to leave his mark upon history. He plans to endow his native Germany with riches from the Orient, to reign over kings and princes, to consume exotic foods, and to wield secret knowledge that will enable him to be, he believes, essentially like God.

But once he takes possession of Mephostophilis as his servant, it becomes quickly apparent that the devil isn't as much serving the morally blind doctor as he is manipulating him. Faustus begins his symbolic 24 years (each year representing an hour of the day) with a tour of the constellations, riding on a "fiery steed" launched from Mount Olympus. Once sated with the stars, he and Mephostophilis visit the academic centers of continental Europe: Paris, Assisi, and Padua, before they descend on Rome to play prankster with Pope Adrian. After invisibly stealing into the Pope's dining chamber on the Feast of the Chair of St. Peter, no less, Faustus tweaks the pontiff's nose and boxes his ears. To his credit, the Holy Father realizes he's in the presence of evil and gets three holy friars to perform an exorcism, by which Faustus and his companion are driven away.

Aside from helping to set free the anti-Pope Bruno and returning him to his native Germany, nothing that Faustus does during his 24 years is significant in any way to the course of human events, or even to his own life. Despite his ambitious designs on being a world ruler, rearranging geography, and becoming extraordinarily wealthy, Dr. Faustus fritters away his 24 years in "pleasure and dalliance"—partaking in meaningless practical jokes like clapping antlers onto the head of a knight he finds offensive, allowing a horse courser to believe that he has pulled Dr. Faustus's leg off, and eating an enormous load of hay in front of a carter, whose livelihood he is undermining.

These 24 years go quickly—not only for Dr. Faustus, but for Marlowe's audience. The script is written in such a way that time speeds up as the play progresses, getting across to us the idea that Faustus has been duped by the devil's empty promises. In the end, it is clear that the prideful professor has traded his soul for nothing.

Then comes the eleventh hour, the final hour of the final day marking the end of his 24-year bargain. Faustus's belief in Hell seems to change dramatically, almost overnight. Whereas he had once convinced himself that Hell was no more than a silly old wives' tale meant to scare people into submission, as his end draws nigh he now abruptly reconsiders that it might be a real place, one where he doesn't want to spend eternity. He acknowledges the reality and fears the pains of Hell. He dances with a kind of imperfect contrition, wondering if it might just be a good idea for him to two-step into repentance. But the devil's influence is complete. Faustus's vicious habits render him a slave to sin. Even as he knows he should repent, he convinces himself that his sins are so great that God can't forgive him. In a word, he despairs—committing the unpardonable sin against the Holy Spirit. At the same time, Faustus believes that if he breaks his pact, the devil will tear him to pieces.

The play ends with an ultimate irony that the sound Christian will easily recognize. During the final scene, the scholars of Wittenburg return to Dr. Faustus's room to find him torn asunder—not because he broke his deal with the devil, but because he kept it!

The end result is that Marlowe's play serves as a timeless cautionary tale, one that has been dramatized in many forms through the centuries, ranging from Bulgokov's *Master and the Margarita* and Wilde's *The Picture of Dorian Gray* to films such as Alan Parker's *Angel Heart* and Roman Polanski's *Rosemary's Baby*. That being said, *The Tragical History of Doctor Faustus* goes far beyond being a mere cautionary tale. Marlowe's play provides an incisive commentary on 21st-century attitudes toward religion and the Church—the idea, for example, that Hell doesn't exist, that it's a mere wives' tale, and that theologians over the past fifty years have spilled much ink trying to rationalize away Christ's warning of eternal perdition. Perhaps most resonant is that a man of such raw intellect, subject to the sin of pride, can become so morally blind that his judgment and logic are impaired beyond remedy.

But the simplest message remains: It's just never a good idea to make a deal with the devil.

"Young Goodman Brown" (1835)
NATHANIEL HAWTHORNE

*I*n the classic format of the Faustian bargain tale, when mortal man makes a deal with the devil, he seeks a well-defined short-term personal gain—knowledge, power, authority, riches—in exchange for a long-term loss, that of his immortal soul. Irving's Tom Walker, Wilde's Dorian Gray, and Marlowe's Doctor Faustus all follow along this narrative: Walker trades his soul in exchange for being the wealthiest man in colonial Massachusetts, Gray for eternal youth and beauty, and Faustus to have Mephistopheles at his beck and call for 24 years of conjuring.

This Faustian-style exchange is not clear, however, in Nathaniel Hawthorne's eminent short story "Young Goodman Brown," set in and around the Puritan village of Salem at the time of the famous witch trials. All we know is that one night a newly married Brown kisses his wife Faith goodnight to carry out an errand with a "present evil purpose" in the nearby woods, the classic literary symbol of descent into darkness as well as the historical site of alleged Satanic crimes for those accused during the Salem Witch Trials of 1692–93. He leaves Faith at the door of their home, dressed in her ostentatiously symbolic pink hair ribbons, telling himself that "after this one night I'll cling to her skirts and follow her to heaven." Young Goodman Brown has made an appointment to meet the devil himself. He has arranged for a Faustian bargain of sorts, but his reason for venturing into the woods on that particular night remains ambiguous. We do know, at the outset, that he believes he can dabble with the devil just this once and then return to Faith spiritually unscathed and continue on his earthly pilgrimage with heaven as his eternal prize. He is fondling sin for some foolish reason unbeknownst to anyone but himself and the devil, who obligingly keeps his promised appointment.

Young Goodman Brown has a well-defined sense of good and evil. He is a Puritan after all, and his religious community has well-defined expectations for him, expectations for citizenship, worship, and moral behavior, expectations that one does not so easily jettison. The devil to the Puritans of Salem is more than merely a spiritual reality; he is a physical manifestation of evil, prowling about the world, seeking the ruin of souls. Brown knows this, but temptation calls to him so strongly that he is willing to leave his Faith behind for what he apparently believes can remain a spiritual one-night stand. What he thinks he has to gain is never clear, never even implied.

What we do know is that once confronted by the devil himself "in grave and decent attire as if he is a respectable member of the town"—we later discover that the devil has come disguised as Young Goodman Brown's long-deceased grandfather—the young Brown has immediate misgivings. He recoils at evil, responding as a man with a well-formed conscience is wont to do. How did I get to this point, he asks himself. Why did I come? "Friend," he says with intended resolve to the devil, "having kept covenant by meeting thee here, it is my purpose now to return whence I came. I have scruples touching the matter."

But Young Goodman Brown is dealing with the master of deception, who convinces him to walk just a little further into the woods with him to discuss the situation, offering his walking staff, which resembles a great black snake that appears to "twist and wriggle itself like a living serpent." As Brown continues to walk with the devil, he regrets that he will be the first in his good Christian family to embark on such an evil errand: "We have been a race of honest men and good Christians since the days of the martyrs; and shall I be the first of the name of Brown that ever took this path?"

From that point, the devil dials up the deception, with an ambiguity deftly dealt by the hand of Hawthorne. As the journey continues deeper into the woods, the reader comes to understand at least partially why Young Goodman Brown has come: There is to be a meeting of a witches' coven to initiate two new young members, one of which will be Brown himself. In response to his misgivings, the devil seeks conveniently to reassure the young Brown. "I have been acquainted with your family as with ever a one among the Puritans," the devil reveals. He tells Young Goodman Brown that both his father and grandfather had been in league with him. He helped his grandfather, a village constable, lash Quaker women through the streets of Salem and helped Brown's father to set fire to an Indian village. But Young Goodman Brown isn't convinced. He still believes that his family are people of prayer and good works and would abide no such wickedness.

All the while, the devil is luring him deeper into the forest, informing Young Goodman Brown that leaders in the church, the government, and the courts are all "firm supporters" of his evil interests. As if to douse Brown's doubts, the devil leaves him on his own for a bit, in the middle of the dark woods, where he first sees Goody Cloyse, the old woman who taught him his catechism, walking on her own. Brown looks on as she converses with the devil, whom she seems to happily recognize. "They tell me there is a nice young man to be taken into communion to-night," Young Goodman overhears her saying to the devil. Soon thereafter, he also sees and hears his own minister and Deacon Gookin, two official representatives of the Puritan hierarchy, walking along the same path—with the same intention: to attend the coven where not one but two new members are to be initiated. The other is said to be "a goodly young woman."

Young Goodman Brown is horrified to discover that Goody Cloyse, Deacon Gookin, and his own minister are in league with the devil. At this point he still has some resolve to repent and return to Faith, his wife. Distraught by these awful revelations, he throws up his hands and cries, "With heaven above and Faith below, I will yet stand firm against the devil!"

But the devil is ready with his response to this resolve. He drives an ominous black cloud between Brown and the heavens, filled with an unseen multitude, the voices of townspeople, many of whom he recognizes, "both saints and sinners," he says. Among those is his own wife.

"Faith! Faith!" yells Young Goodman Brown, after which "something fluttered lightly through the air and caught on the branch of a tree"—a pink ribbon, which he takes as a sign of his wife. This is the turning point for Young Goodman Brown, the point at which he gives up and despairs, believing his wife to be a part of this evil. "My Faith is gone!" he cries out in double entendre. "Come, devil, for to thee is this world given."

From that point on, the devil's work is an easy task. Leading his initiate out further into the woods, the devil takes him to a clearing surrounded by four blazing pines that reveal a multitudinous congregation looking. Among them, Young Goodman Brown recognizes "faces that would be seen the next day at the council board of the province, and others which, Sabbath after Sabbath, looked devoutly heavenward, and benignantly over the crowded pews, from the holiest pulpits of the land"—in short, the leaders of church and government whom Young Goodman Brown has revered since his youth.

And then the bewildered young man beholds his own wife, who is being led out as he is to be initiated into communion with this devilish congregation. "Faith! Faith!" cries the husband. "Look up to heaven, and resist the wicked one." With that, he finds himself alone in the woods "in the coldest dew," with no evidence that any of these surrounding pines had ever been on fire.

Yes, Young Goodman Brown does appear to have agreed to meet the devil in the woods to be initiated into some devilish group populated by the so-called saints of Salem; yet no such group truly exists beyond that conjured as a devilish deception, one that certainly achieved its purpose: claiming the soul of Young Goodman Brown, because, after that night, "a distrustful, if not a desperate man did he become from the night of that fearful dream."

The young Brown, however, his judgement clouded by seeking out sin, is unable to discern the deception. He believes what he's seen. He believes the leaders of the community are all in league with the devil, even as he is unable to see that it is he alone in this case who is in league with the forces of darkness. The deception has had its desired effect. Young Goodman Brown turns away from Faith and from all goodness, and instead looks at everyone upon his return to Salem village in the morning with grave suspicion. He sees himself as the lone righteous citizen, believing he has succeeded in turning away from sin in the woods. Like the accusers of the historical Salem, everyone was a potential witch if it suited their purposes. They were certain of nothing in those days but their own righteousness, which they saw as unimpeachable. Indeed, no good comes from Young Goodman Brown's own self-righteousness. For he can no longer pray or sing hymns or listen to preaching about the Bible: "When the minister spoke from the pulpit with power and fervid eloquence, and with his hand on the open Bible, of the sacred truths for our religion, and of saint-like lives and triumphant deaths, and of future bliss or misery unutterable, then did Goodman Brown turn pale, dreading lest the roof should thunder down upon the gray blasphemer and his hearers."

He cannot even trust Faith, his own wife. Upon his return to the village, Young Goodman Brown "spied the head of Faith, with the pink ribbons, gazing anxiously forth, and bursting into such joy at the sight of him, that she skipped along the street and almost kissed him," but her husband is having none of it. He only looks sternly into her face and passes on without even greeting her. The devil's deception is complete. Young Goodman Brown trusts no one for the remainder of his long, lonely life.

Although we can see what the devil gets in this bargain, nothing is gained—no worldly power, excessive riches, fame, or beauty—for the despairing Young Goodman Brown: "And when he had lived long and was borne to his grave...they carved no hopeful verse upon his tombstone; for his dying hour was gloom."

PART TWO

Transhumanist Goals

PERFECTION, COMFORT, & IMMORTALITY

Brave New World (1932)

ALDOUS HUXLEY

*H*elmholtz Watson is an alpha-plus male in Aldous Huxley's dystopic *Brave New World*. Broad-shouldered, deep-chested, tall, attractive to the ladies, and respected by other well-endowed males in his elite caste, Helmholtz is a lecturer at the College of Emotional Engineering (CEE). His job: sloganeering. He's a sort of reductive, futuristic Madison Avenue man. But rather than pushing products for slick corporations, he is a prime player in the World State's ubiquitous social conditioning program known as hypnopaedia, or "sleep teaching."

Helmholtz's only creative task at the CEE is to compose pithy slogans that can be readily absorbed and regurgitated by the masses. Once devised, these slogans are piped into the ears of sleeping children who invariably come to accept them as undeniable truths and repeat them to one another in place of authentic conversation. Ironically, given the superficiality of Huxley's society, these hypnopeadic proverbs are heavily laden with World State propaganda, and their use is intended primarily to diffuse anything but the most anodyne conversations.

For the reader, these proverbs are also an efficient means to apprehend the precepts that undergird Huxley's imagined (but eerily familiar) futuristic dystopia, wherein its citizens are manipulated not by force and tyranny but by constant amusement and pleasure: "When the individual feels, the community reels" and "Everyone belongs to everyone else" indicate the Marxist penchant to jettison individual human dignity in favor of an ersatz common good, including pervasive sexual promiscuity from age five and up; "Ending is better than mending" and "The more stitches, the less riches" ungrammatically reflect the World State's self-indulgent consumerist mentality; "Never put off tomorrow the fun you can have today" captures its culture of hedonism and instant gratification; "History is bunk" sums up the Modernist attitude toward the past, one that views historical facts as unpleasant and seeks to minimize the influence of wisdom, tradition, and culture. Most importantly, perhaps, the universal use of the happy pill *soma* is encapsulated in gems like "A gramme is better than a damn" and "One cubic centimeter cures ten gloomy sentiments." Why deal with unpleasant emotions like anger, fear, or sadness when you can pop a pill to take you away from your quotidian cares?

Although Helmholtz Watson has everything the World State has to offer a man in this brave new world, he senses he's missing something important, something essential to his very being. In the early chapters of Huxley's prescient novel, Helmholtz flirts with the seemingly far-fetched concept that he is an individual capable of independent thought, as unorthodox an idea in the World State as any. When he shares his suspicions with the novel's unlikable gadfly anti-hero, Bernard Marx, the plot unfolds with the typical dystopian trope of unorthodox man versus society. Helmholtz and Bernard decide to rebel against the World State, each in his own way, but both inspired by the nagging belief that there's more to this life than simply amusing themselves to death.

What Helmholtz desires, but is not yet able to articulate, is to use his genetically engineered (but still human) talents to write authentically from the heart, capturing and appealing to the wide range of human emotions, rather than merely turning out soundbite propaganda. What he's ultimately seeking is a way to become human in his dehumanizing world, where every aspect of society is designed to encourage him to live a life of the utmost superficiality and turn him away from anything that would give him pause to be introspective.

What he—and nearly everyone else in *Brave New World*—lacks is human dignity, and that's exactly how the World State wants it. When a society's citizens lack human dignity they become subjects easily manipulated and controlled. The leaders of the brave new world facilitate this manipulation and control through genetic engineering for the manufacture of children *in vitro*, social conditioning, propaganda, psychotropic drugs that give people immediate happiness, and instant gratification of sensory desires. They have successfully learned to become tyrants through pleasure rather than by force. Mustapha Mond, one of a handful of World Controllers, explains to Helmholtz (after Helmholtz gets hauled in for helping to incite a riot at a *soma* distribution center), that the ultimate goal of society is universal happiness, even if it means that truth and beauty and knowledge must be sacrificed. Consequently, God and the worship of God, along with religious observance and devotion, must be eliminated at all cost. With God comes goodness, beauty, and truth, Mustapha Mond explains in a moment of transparency as he is sentencing Helmholtz to banishment. "God is not compatible with machinery and scientific medicine and universal happiness."

And Christianity, he says, was also incompatible with universal happiness. It required self-control and sacrifice and sometimes resulted in suffering—all of which are anathema in the brave new world. So, we jettisoned Christianity long ago, he explains, in favor of self-indulgence and unrestricted copulation: "You can't have a lasting civilization without plenty of vices." Forget the noble and fine and heroic exemplified by centuries of Christian saints, he says, because "civilization has absolutely no need for nobility or heroism. These things are symptoms of political inefficiency. In a properly organized society like ours, nobody has any opportunities for being noble or heroic. Conditions have got to be thoroughly unstable before the occasion can arise." To Mustapha Mond, Christianity means divided allegiances, temptations to be resisted, objects of love to be fought for and defended—in a word, instability. In our brave new world, Mond tells Helmholtz, "There's no such thing as divided allegiance; you're so conditioned that you can't help doing what you ought to do. And what you ought to do is on the whole, so many of the natural impulses are allowed free play, that there really aren't any temptations to resist." Of course, if anything ever does arise, one can always resort to *soma* "to calm your anger, to reconcile you to your enemies, to make you patient and longsuffering." *Soma*, Mond adds, is "Christianity without tears."

It's instructive to note, however, that religious observance and devotion isn't simply eliminated from the World State. It's merely transformed, gutted of its truth and beauty and replaced with superficial self-indulgence. Jesus Christ, for example, is replaced by Henry Ford, who is seen as the "savior" of this society of perpetual happiness due to his invention of the assembly line, which has been adapted for the manufacture of children in the World State. The Sign of the Cross has been replaced with the "Sign of the T" (as in Ford's Model T), which citizens make reverently over their bellies at secularly appropriate times; "Our Ford" replaces Our Lord; and the Christian dating system has become the Fordian dating system, the year A. F. 141 meaning 141 years after the death of Henry Ford.

Just as the many sacred houses of Christian worship in our own 21st century have been secularized into condos, restaurants, and brew pubs, Westminster Abbey, that iconic house of worship for the Church of England and the British aristocracy, is now a World State cabaret and dance hall, emblazoned by giant neon signs advertising "London's Finest Scent and Colour Organ, All the Latest Synthetic Music," and "Calvin Stopes and His Sixteen Sexophonists." Hundreds of couples five-step around the polished floor each weekend to tunes with insipid lyrics such as "There ain't no Bottle in all the world like that dear little bottle of mine," a doggerel verse homage to the wonders of *soma*.

The Church of England's hierarchy has undergone a secularization as well. The former title of Archbishop of Canterbury, for example, is now the Arch-Community Songster, currently held by a charismatic old fellow who seems to do little more than cruise *soma* parties looking for sexual companions.

Those former churches that have not been converted to nightclubs or brewpubs are now known as Fordson Community Singeries, the sites of "Ford's Day celebrations and other massed Community Sings." It is here where the World State's most bizarre secularized religious ritual takes place on alternate Thursdays. Known as *Solidarity Services*, these fortnight gatherings feature a group of twelve—yes, as in twelve disciples—under the tutelage of a Solidarity President, gathered around a table in a perfect Solidarity Circle—man, woman, man, woman: "Twelve of them ready to be made one, waiting to come together, to be fused, to lose their twelve separate identities in a larger being."

If that's not enough to convince you this is a mocking of the Mass, consider the ritual itself: The President stands up and makes the sign of the T, plays canned music—the soft beating and pulsing rhythms of plan-gently repeated drums—that functions as the entrance hymn. Then the President sits down, and a communal strawberry shake laced with *soma* is passed from hand to hand, each of the communicants responding with "I drink to my annihilation." After singing two Solidarity Hymns, each comprised of twelve yearning stanzas with howlers such as "Ford, we are twelve; oh, make us one, like drops within the Social River," the inner light of universal happiness breaks out on every face in saccharine smiles. But the true communion has not been achieved until the group reaches a kind of altered consciousness that ends in everyone sharing themselves with everyone else, succinctly expressed in a final verse set to the thumping of tom-toms: "Orgy-porgy, Ford and fun, / Kiss the girls and make them One. / Boys at one with girls at peace; Orgy-porgy gives release."

And, well, that pretty much sums up the self-indulgent sexualized world of *Brave New World*. Eliminate religion, truth, beauty, goodness. Jettison the family in favor of the State. Gratify everyone's every desire as quickly as possible, condition them to hate history, keep them amused with sex, soma, screens, and sports. Provide them with propaganda soundbites to live by. And kill and cremate them when they turn sixty so that no one becomes old and flabby and wrinkly.

If we're being honest with ourselves, we'll easily recognize Huxley's imagined world in our own contemporary society where the decerebrated masses uncritically follow a media narrative, repeat mindless slogans, ceaselessly watch spectator sports, engage in endless hours of screen time, follow sporting events religiously, and immerse themselves in various forms of pornography and sexual promiscuity on a grand scale—each and every one of these typical 21st-century pursuits. Add in the expunging of God, the denigration of marriage, the dissolution of the family, and the anti-life initiatives of today's biotechnology revolution, and one can easily read Aldous Huxley's *Brave New World* not merely as a cautionary tale but as a plethora of prophecies come true.

Like all great literature, however, it's not the simple fact that Huxley was prophetic; rather it's that he is able to articulate, however clumsily, for generation after generation, through the medium of an engaging narrative, the underlying philosophies—be it of Marxism or Freudianism or Modernism—that will in any century dehumanize us and lead us away from God and all that is truly good and beautiful, all that gives meaning to our lives and makes us authentically human.

And this is precisely what bothers Helmholtz Watson. Even with his genetic engineering, his Neo-Pavlovian conditioning, his soma usage, and his participation in the World State's carefully designed atonement rituals, he is still aware of his own humanity, and by the end of the novel he does succeed in getting what he wants: a life of writing alone in a poor climate (the Falkland Islands), without the use of *soma*, and all the time on the world to produce great literature. The sad part of Helmholtz's success, however, is that he'll be writing great literature for no one, because there's no one left with the desire to read or the ability to appreciate great art.

Gulliver's Travels (1726)

JONATHAN SWIFT

*I*n 1726, essayist and poet Jonathan Swift published his magnum opus, now regarded as an indisputable classic of English literature. *Gulliver's Travels* is both a satire on human nature and a parody of popular travel narratives of his day. Swift's satirical fury—Thackeray called it "furious, raging, obscene"—is directed against almost every aspect of early-18th-century life. Lemuel Gulliver, a practical-minded English surgeon-turned-captain of the high seas, sets sail in his aptly named ship, The Adventure, to visit "several remote nations of the world."

The most well-known scene of Swift's satirical tour de force is Gulliver's shipwreck on the island of Lilliput, inhabited by a race of six-inch-tall little people who enjoy arguing over trivial matters such as whether boiled eggs ought to be cracked open at the big end or little end, a clever parody of British political and religious disputes of his day. It is here on the shores of Lilliput where the brave traveler wakes to finds himself a god-like giant bound by a thousand tiny threads, addressed by his Lilliputian captors, who regard him with awe—and later use him as their personal Goliath to subdue the neighboring Blefuscudians. Swift's satire is on full display when the giant Gulliver is charged with treason for publicly urinating in the capital, even though he was doing so in order to put out a raging Lilliputian fire.

Later, in the kingdom of Brobdingnag, Gulliver (like Lewis Carroll's 19th-century Alice) finds the tables have turned. Here, he is a tiny man in a country of giants where he is treated as a zoological curiosity and exhibited for money. Through Gulliver's subsequent experiences with the philosopher citizens on the flying island of Laputa, Swift spoofs the speculations of contemporary science. The Laputans are so obsessed by theoretical science—they contemplate ways to extract sunbeams from cucumbers, for example—that they have to be reminded to listen and speak to one another. Then there's the land of the virtuous horse-like Houyhnhnms whom Swift uses to contrast to the Yahoos, vicious brutes who bear a disturbing resemblance to humans.

In one of the lesser sensationalized episodes in his travels to fantastical foreign lands, Gulliver recounts his visit to the island kingdom of Luggnagg, where every few years a child is born with a distinctive circular birthmark on the forehead that infallibly indicates that he or she will never die. When Gulliver first learns of these "struldbrugs" from mortal Luggnaggians, he is "struck with an inexpressible delight" and cries out in rapture, "Happy nation, where every child hath at least a chance of being immortal!" Gulliver admits that, before his visit to Luggnagg, he had regarded death as the "universal calamity of human nature," the cause of "depression of spirits" due to the "continued apprehension of death." This view changes, however, when he eventually learns the truth about the immoral struldbrugs.

Amused by Gulliver's enthusiasm, the mortal Luggnaggians ask him to describe how he would live if it had fallen to his lot to be born an immortal. Gulliver imagines the good fortune: He would procure himself riches, apply himself to the perpetual study of all arts and sciences, and carefully record history as it unfolds before him, from age to age. "I should be a living treasury of knowledge and wisdom, and certainly become the oracle of the nation," he delightfully asserts, imagining himself dedicated to educating generation after generation of "hopeful young men."

Gulliver also imagines he would organize a united brotherhood of his fellow immortals who would be his constant companions. Together, he says, they would draw on their collective experience and observation through the centuries to counsel mankind to reject the various ways corruption steals into the world, which would prevent "continual degeneracy of human nature, so justly complained of in all ages." At the same time, Gulliver admits that he may well grow to accept the ongoing loss of mortal friends and family with as little regret as mortals feel for the withering of annual flowers.

The mortal Luggnaggians politely listen to Gulliver riff on the virtues of his speculative human immortality, smiling at his desire for endless life and sublunary happiness. But they soon set their visitor straight. Though they are immortal, the struldbrugs enjoy neither perpetual youth nor perpetual prosperity, health, and vigor. Gulliver's interpreter explains that the question put to him "was not whether a man would choose to be always in the prime of youth, attended with prosperity and health; but how he would pass a perpetual life under the usual disadvantages old age brings along with it." The lot of the struldbrugs is reminiscent of Homer's Tithonus: When Eos asks Zeus to make Tithonus immortal, she forgets to ask that he be granted eternal youth to go with it. Tithonus indeed lives forever, "but when loathsome old age pressed full upon him, and he could not move nor lift his limbs, this seemed to her in her heart the best counsel: she laid him in a room and put to the shining doors. There he babbles endlessly, and no more has strength at all, such as once he had in his supple limbs."

Like Tithonus, Swift's struldbrugs live anything but enviable lives. Around the age of 30, they begin to grow increasingly melancholy and dejected, arising from the dreadful prospect of never dying. Through no fault of their own, they are condemned to a perpetual continuance in the world. Consequently, they become envious of the mortals among them: "Whenever they see a funeral, they lament and repine that others are gone to an harbor of rest, to which they themselves never can hope to arrive."

By the time they reach eighty years of age, their marriages are dissolved, their children take their inheritances, and the state strips them of all rights of citizenship. Only a small pittance is set aside for their perpetual care in old age, and they become wards of the state. For the same reason that the Vatican takes away papal voting rights for cardinals over age eighty, Luggnagg's royal court has decided that, by that age, struldbrugs have lost the cognitive ability of right reason. Many of the struldbrugs entirely lose their memories or can remember only what they observed in their youth and middle age. They can no longer recall the names of persons, even those who are their nearest friends and relatives. By age ninety, they lose their teeth and hair, and the ability to taste, "but eat and drink whatever they can get, without relish or appetite, possibly an homage to the final stage of Shakespeare's seven ages of man ("*sans* teeth, *sans* eyes, *sans* taste, *sans* everything"). After two hundred years, because language invariably changes so much in that time, the poor old struldbrugs can no longer communicate with any of the contemporary mortals, who seem to them to be speaking in a foreign tongue.

> The harsh reality, Gulliver observes after meeting several struldbrugs in the flesh, is that they are universally despised even from birth. "They were the most mortifying sight I ever beheld... Besides the usual deformities in extreme old age, they acquired an additional ghastliness, in proportion to their number of years, which is not to be described," observes Gulliver with as much distaste as any throughout all his travels in The Adventure. "No tyrant could invent a death into which I would not run with pleasure from such a life," he admits.

The reality of Swift's struldbrugs inspires consideration of the abiding human passion to indefinitely prolong human life in the pursuit of immortality. Yes, long life is a universal desire of mankind, regardless of time and culture. Yet one of the most important characteristics of human nature is that we are mortal. Our life on this earth is finite. We will all meet death in one way or another, whether after years of earthly bedridden suffering or suddenly, like a thief in the night. That's the primary reason that the inevitability of death is one of the most universally explored themes in literature. To prolong the inevitable is a fool's errand, one that denies another universal truth: the existence of the immortal human soul and consequently the immortal afterlife. Contrary to the thinking of many, death is not the greatest human evil. It is a blessing, one that leads to the eternal afterlife united with the Creator. It's also a keen motivator to pursue living a good life, which is more or less what Gulliver describes when asked about how he might live if born immortal and what our classical philosophers taught when promoting the pursuit of a life well-lived.

Unlike those wise ancient thinkers, the transhumanists of our day find it difficult to accept the reality of the eternal human soul. They can't see it, touch it, or measure it. And so, death remains for them, in the words of Gulliver, "the universal calamity of human nature," and must be stopped at all costs. For them, earthly death is the end—a sort of "game over." That may explain why transhumanists like Ray Kurzweil imagine a future world in which death is a preventable evil or, in his words, "an elective procedure." Kurzweil and his fellow travelers explore their immortality project through the use of nanotechnology, cryotechnology, psychoactive drugs, DNA backups, brain transplants, and digital uploading of the mind—all speculative procedures dramatized in recent science fiction films and television shows.

This philosophy, in its general principles, is shared by many these days who would hardly consider themselves transhumanists. Medical professionals, for example, are dedicated to the proposition that anything that promises to prolong life is unequivocally a good thing. They consequently celebrate any technology that appears to put off death, regardless of impact to quality of life or ethical considerations concerning the dignity of the human person. The biotech industry, for example, is already in a race to find a genetic shortcut to immortality, using controversial embryonic stem cell research and human cloning, including the patenting of human genes. It's too early to tell whether the biotech industry will eventually be able to offer an easy solution to life extension, but it seems reasonable to assume that the cumulative research in this area will result in increasing life-expectancies over time. The fact remains, here and now, that most medical technologies keep people's bodies alive at a much reduced quality of life. That, in part, explains the increasing demands for assisted suicide and euthanasia rights. But it also raises a question tangentially broached in *Gulliver's Travels*: If the struldbrugs were to remain healthy and prosperous as they aged, would they necessarily be happy, having avoided the pitfalls of old age? Lemuel Gulliver seems to think so, imagining himself as an immortal font of human knowledge and culture, almost God-like in his wisdom and historical omniscience. But Gulliver clearly hasn't weighed the pros and cons of immortal youth; nor has he considered its unintended consequences. An essential part of being human is physical mortality, which itself has ramifications for how we live our lives, view our relationships, thrive in marriage and family life, and strive to succeed through industry and innovation. This very concept has been explored in many "fountain of youth" stories in every age. Perhaps the most direct and incisive exploration of these related questions of eternal youth is Nathalie Babbit's *Tuck Everlasting* (1975), the story of a family who unwittingly drinks from a secret stream that renders them ageless and immortal. Miles, who was 22 years old when he drank from the miraculous waters, laments that he has been long estranged from his children who are now in their eighties. "You can't have living without dying," he tells a mortal friend who's just discovered his secret. And even though he's living perpetually in the prime of youth, Miles likens the immortals of his family to "rocks beside the road"—meaning that by losing their mortality, they've also lost their humanity.

Gulliver's visit to Luggnagg also illustrates nicely why Swift's satire is timeless. Not only did it resonate with his peers in the early eighteenth century, but it still resonates today. The primary target of criticism here is societal attitudes toward the elderly. By using the hyperbolic example of the struldbrugs, Swift points out an ugly truth of his time and ours: We often treat the elderly with profound disrespect and generally view them not as a source of wisdom or a living font from which cultural knowledge can easily flow from one generation to the next; rather, we pay caretakers to shut them away from their families and friends, and then look on them as a drain on financial resources. Our world is a world that is youth-obsessed. We seem to have little value for wisdom and little understanding of the value of human life in its twilight years.

Swift's satire asks us to reconsider some of the assumptions we have about both life and death. Although made in the image and likeness of God, we are mortal beings for a reason—so that we may prepare in this life for the eternal bliss of life in the next. Anyone who understands the promises of heaven would be a fool to exchange that life for interminable suffering here in this valley of tears.

"The Birth-mark" (1843)

NATHANIEL HAWTHORNE

*M*an has long been alive to the many ways in which our bodies decay and perish, the ways our bodies are fallible and imperfect. But unique among God's creatures, we also have the power of imagination and consequently the ability to shape our environment and ourselves. With that power, although far from omnipotent, comes responsibility. One of the oldest continuing moral dilemmas, in fact, concerns our response to the questions of human mortality and imperfection. Should we aspire to indefinitely extend human life? Should we try to mold our imperfections by using our human ingenuity and genius? In other words, should man aspire to control Nature? Should man aspire to play God?

One of Nathaniel Hawthorne's many compelling short stories perfectly captures this ancient dilemma. "The Birth-mark" is the tale of Aylmer, a late-19th-century idealist scientist whose love for science rivals his love for his wife. Georgiana is an otherwise perfectly beautiful young woman with a small hand-shaped birthmark on her left cheek. One day, soon after their wedding Aylmer asks Georgiana, "Has it ever occurred to you that the mark upon your cheek might be removed?" This shocks his wife because, as she explains, she's always thought of it as a charm, as much a part of herself as the rest of her body. In fact many a man, it is said, "would have risked life for the privilege of pressing his lips to the mysterious hand."

What seems at first like an insignificant and offhand question, albeit a loutish one, quickly escalates to an obsession. Aylmer wants the birthmark, that "tint of deeper crimson," removed from his wife's face. He says he wants Georgiana as perfect as Pygmalion's marble Galatea: "Seeing her otherwise so perfect, he found this one defect grow more and more intolerable with every moment of their united lives." (Recall that Pygmalion was a misogynist sculptor who found women so unattractive that he made a "perfect" one out of stone.) Every conversation during their honeymoon period is tainted by Aylmer's obsession. He invariably reverts to this one topic every time he sees his wife. In fact, it doesn't seem that he sees Georgiana at all, but rather he sees her birthmark: "With the morning twilight Aylmer opened his eyes upon his wife's face and recognized the symbol of imperfection; and when they sat together at the evening hearth his eyes wandered stealthily to her cheek, and beheld, flickering with the blaze of wood fire, the spectral hand that wrote mortality." As the obsession progresses, Aylmer begins to draw back in disgust at the sight of the birthmark. He is convinced that he should correct what Nature left imperfect, and he devotes his every waking hour to concocting just the right potion that will do the trick. This birthmark is no superficial blemish, easily removed, like a mole. No, Aylmer tells Georgiana, her hand-shaped birthmark runs deep, intertwined into her very fabric.

In fact, Aylmer is so obsessed with making his wife "perfect" that he talks in his sleep one night. The next day, Georgiana asks her husband if he remembers the dream. "A terrible dream!" she explains, "I wonder that you can forget it. Is it possible to forget this one expression? 'It is in her heart now; we must have it out!'" With Georgiana's prodding, Aylmer recalls his dream—obvious foreshadowing—of operating on his wife's face, an operation for the removal of the birthmark: "But the deeper went the knife, the deeper sank the hand, until at length its tiny grasp appeared to have caught hold of Georgiana's heart; whence, however, her husband was inexorably resolved to cut or wrench it away."

Georgiana is understandably none too happy. She begins to shudder at his gaze, and eventually she becomes so self-conscious that she too desires that the birthmark be removed, if only to please her husband. But Georgiana is astute. She prays that, "for a single moment," she might satisfy Aylmer's deepest desire. Longer than one moment she knows it cannot be, "for his spirit was ever on the march, ever ascending, and each instant required something that was beyond the scope of the instant before."

Much of the story recounts the many experiments Aylmer the scientist undertakes, nearly all of them failures, en route to discovering exactly how to conquer the birthmark. Some might classify Aylmer in the category of the mad scientist, the man who with complete disregard for the dignity of the human person, presses on in his experiments in the name of discovery and invention, with a sole eye toward advancing his own reputation as a groundbreaking scientist. That may be so. But, more importantly perhaps, Aylmer is a man acting on the vice of pride, of overreaching ambition. As the medieval philosophers might say, "vice ravages reason," and in Aylmer's case, his pride has transformed him into an unreasonable man. Even after demonstrating to Georgiana the effects of his elixir of life on a plant, he still believes his own carefully brewed concoction will provide the proper "treatment" for Georgiana. It is instructive to note that, although Aylmer was able to make the plant grow exceedingly fast and unfold a beautiful flower, the whole plant suffered a blight and died.

Aylmer becomes so obsessed, his reason so ravished, he tells Georgiana that he now rejoices in the single imperfection of her birthmark, "since it will be such a rapture to remove it." And a rapture it is! After much labor over failed experiments, Aylmer gives Georgiana his magic concoction, using his wife as the subject of his latest experiment. "Drink, then, thou lofty creature!" he says, handing her a goblet. She drinks, and—much to Aylmer's intense glee—the crimson hand begins to fade from his wife's cheek. And indeed it continues to fade until Georgiana's cheek is "perfect." But as the cheek fades, so does Georgiana. "My peerless bride," exclaims the delighted scientist, "it is successful! You are perfect!" But as you might already have guessed, although the experiment is a success (the birthmark has been removed), the patient dies, the ultimate of unintended consequences to his god-like overreaching. Aylmer gets his desire fulfilled. That sole token of human imperfection fades from his wife's cheek—and Georgiana, in his eyes, is made perfect—but at what cost? His wife is dead, and therefore perfect only in death, immortal only in death.

On the whole, "The Birth-mark" is both a compelling look at the scientific tendency to overreach its limits and a tragic illustration of the character of one who is tempted to use science this way. Aylmer is a selfish and unloving person who loves his idealistic vision more than he loves his wife or anyone else for that matter. Because of this tragic flaw, Aylmer is unable to understand what is actually good for the woman he is supposed to love. After all, this woman is the man's wife—and as it turns out, Hawthorne might have something to say about a husband's treatment of his wife, looking at her as something to be manipulated for his own ends rather than a person with human dignity to be loved and cherished beyond all but God.

That Hideous Strength (1945)
C. S. LEWIS

*S*ham journalism, fake news, engineered social chaos, the destruction of property rights, incipient total-itarian rule, and the serial misuse of the word "science"—it sounds a lot like America in the 2020s, but it's also the fictional fabric of C. S. Lewis's *That Hideous Strength*, the final novel in his lesser-known *Space Trilogy*, penned during the war years of the early 1940s. The novel follows the moral descent and recovery of Mark Studdock, a promising young professor of the "Progressive Element" at the fictitious University of Edgestow in the imagined years following the Second World War. A sociologist by training and an academic by temperament, Mark is recruited by the influential Lord Feverstone to join the National Institute of Co-ordinated Experiments (N. I. C. E.), a prestigious fledgling organization of top-tier scientists that has recently moved into Edgestow, a quaint English village whose size and beauty are quickly crushed by the institutional jugger-naut. When the university sells land to the N. I. C. E. and invites the Institute to be incorporated into the university, no one at Edgestow is quite sure what the N. I. C. E. is or intends to do once arriving on campus. However, the fact that the N. I. C. E. involves the bustling work of scientists, worshipped back in the 1940s as much as they are today, is enough to extend a collegial warm welcome.

As Mark's recruitment unfolds, he discovers that the N. I. C. E. is Britain's "first attempt to take applied science seriously from the national point of view." The Institution marks the beginning of a new era, he is told, "the *really* scientific era"—an era in which science becomes the national idol. The N. I. C. E. is ostensibly an "instrument" that intends to use "science" in order to solve social problems—the unemployment problem, the cancer problem, the housing problem, the problems of currency, of war, of education—all backed by the whole force of the state. In other words, Feverstone explains, the N. I. C. E. will use the justification of "science" (more accurately that which is *passed off* as science) to control the social order, to "create a new type of man." How to get there? "At first—sterilization of the unfit, liquidation of backward races, selective breeding. Then the real education, including pre-natal education," Feverstone continues. "It'll have to be mainly psychological first. But we'll get onto biological conditioning in the end and direct manipulation of the brain."

Mark is now fascinated. The aims of the N. I. C. E. appear to align perfectly with his own moral and sociological convictions, and the implicit promise of power and control is irresistible, especially when Mark can rationalize that it's all for the betterment of society and the evolutionary improvement of mankind—at least from his Leftist perspective, a perspective that Lewis takes great care to satirize with light-hearted humor throughout the novel. At the same time, Mark is perhaps too young, too naïve, too inexperienced with the wiles of the world to realize that this same "power and control" that now tempts him will necessarily become his own moral straitjacket, one that will force him to keep doing the bidding of the N. I. C. E. no matter what immoral path the Institute's "science" will lead him down, no matter what moral misgivings might begin to prick even his ill-formed conscience.

Eventually Mark realizes that he's been brought on to the N. I. C. E. not as a sociologist to "do science" but as a professional propagandist, one whose duty is to camouflage the Institute's motivations and goals by writing misleading "articles for the educated in the papers read by educated people," since, as it is explained to him, "it's the educated reader who can be gulled.... They'll believe anything." In fact, says Feverstone, the so-called educated class has long been "conditioned" so well that they couldn't stop reading the high-brow papers if they wanted to, a situation not dissimilar to NPR listeners, CNN watchers, and *New York Times* readers of our own day and age who take their "news" as daily gospel. If they hear it on NPR or read it in the *Times,* they believe it. No questions asked. As for the men and women of Lewis's working class in the late 1940s, they take it for granted that the news articles are propaganda and skip right to the football scores. It will be more work to re-condition the proletariat, Feverstone admits. But once the "educated" all fall into line, everyone else will eventually follow along like good sheep.

Mark has no experience as a propagandist but he's a quick study, put under the tutelage of Fairy Hardcastle, the Chief of the N. I. C. E.'s institutional police force, a kind of fledgling Gestapo. First he learns that he must habituate himself to abusing the word "science." By doing so, he will find it easy to justify and garner support for even the most sordid and unpalatable plans, and that includes placing universal restrictions on civil liberties—all, of course, "for the sake of the common good." According to N. I. C. E. wisdom and the folk wisdom of our own time: Who could possibly object if we're just "following the science"? And for those who do object, they will be relegated to the genus of anti-science bumpkin, blamed for obstructing societal progress due to their selfishness, ignorance, and misplaced piety.

Though Mark struggles at first with accepting this transition from academic social scientist to his new role as "journalist" (as he calls himself), he finds intrinsic satisfaction once he realizes the influence of his words.

Formerly, his articles appeared only in learned periodicals read by a handful of his academic peers, but now his N. I. C. E. propaganda is being read by the millions. And how does Mark suddenly have access to writing for all the major British newspapers? The N. I. C. E., of course. The Institute feeds the publishers and editors with a steady diet of cash that allows the N. I. C. E. to control the news any way it desires. In effect, it controls all the nation's newspapers but one—and the one that can't be bought off is crushed by a N. I. C. E.-engineered printers' strike.

Little by little, Mark sheds what few scruples he has in order to create news stories designed to manipulate public opinion in the N. I. C. E.'s favor. However, the turning point in his propaganda career comes when Chief Hardcastle wants Mark to write about the riot in Edgestow—a riot that hasn't happened yet, a riot that will be engineered by the N. I. C. E. in order to vilify the locals. Up to this point, since the N. I. C. E.'s arrival on campus, the Institute has wreaked havoc on the town's daily life especially due to the thousands of N. I. C. E.-contracted construction workers who have moved in to Edgestow. The locals, who figured the Institute workmen were there simply to construct an institutional building, are furious to discover that the plan includes deforestation of the trees surrounding the town, the destruction of a centuries-old Norman church, the requisition of some residential homes, and even the diversion of the Wynd River along which the town was built two hundred years earlier. This influx of the N. I. C. E. population has also created unwieldy crowds and an astronomical increase in crime and violence.

Curiously, none of the N. I. C. E.-induced violence is ever reported in the daily London newspapers or even in the local *Edgestow Telegraph*; this is precisely because it does not fit the institutional narrative. Keep in mind: the N. I. C. E. controls the media. In just the first few days of the N. I. C. E. arrival, there is an "indecent assault" on one of the main streets, two "beatings-up" in a pub, and dozens of complaints of threatening and disorderly behavior. But, again, reports of these ugly incidents never appear in the papers. Instead, residents are surprised to read in the *Telegraph* that the new Institute is "settling down very comfortably in Edgestow and the most cordial relations developing between the N. I. C. E. and town natives"—the exact opposite of the reality Edgestow residents have witnessed, reminding the 2020 reader of the rioting, looting, arson, and statue destruction that took place in many major American cities this summer, all of which was universally described by the likes of NPR, CNN, and the *New York Times* as "peaceful protests" in response to "systemic police racism" following the death of George Floyd, a convicted violent criminal who actually died in police custody of a Fentanyl overdose.

But back to Mark. He is now being called upon not merely to twist or manipulate the news to curry public favor but to concoct the news itself. Since beginning his tenure as a N. I. C. E. propagandist, this riot assignment is the first thing Mark has been asked to do which he himself clearly knows to be unethical and immoral even before he does it. Mark is navigating the slippery slope, well on his way to becoming a bona fide scoundrel. In writing his editorialized news copy about the engineered riot, the endgame is to create a reason for deploying the N. I. C. E. police force to Edgestow to replace the "ordinary police" who are being portrayed as unequal to the task of keeping the peace. Hardcastle makes this clear: The N. I. C. E. wants absolute control of every aspect of the town. The modus operandi here is to engineer chaos so that "emergency regulations" might be put into place—all, of course, for "the sake of the common good"—an abuse of the phrase, to be sure. In his first concocted article about the riot, Mark writes: "If any doubt as to the value of such a force existed, it has been amply set at rest by the episodes at Edgestow.... But for the N. I. C. E. Police, things would have taken quite a different turn." In his second article, a blustering opinion piece, he writes, "We expect from [the N. I. C. E.] a brighter, cleaner and fuller life for our children, in which we and they can march ever onward and onward and develop to the full urge of life which God has given each one of us. The N. I. C. E. is the people's instrument for bringing about all the things we fought for [in the Second World War]." Mark's overall argument is that no honest citizen would ever stand in the way of these "virtuous" N. I. C. E. goals; to do so would be anti-social and un-patriotic.

Not content to simply concoct news for the sake of manipulating public opinion, Mark also vilifies the opposition—the longtime local residents—by imputing to them false motives and false actions. In one of his "fake news" articles, Mark makes it sound as if the riot was engineered not by the N. I. C. E. but by local residents who object to the Institute's presence in Edgestow. "I say these disturbances have been engineered," Mark writes. "The people of England are not going to stand this. We are not going to have the Institute sabotaged. What is to be done at Edgestow? I say put the whole place under the Institutional Police.... It doesn't make sense to expect these poor old Bobbies to deal with an engineered riot. Last night the N. I. C. E. police showed that they could. Give them a free hand and let them get on with the job."

It is worth noting that Lewis's descriptions of the actual Edgestow riot bear a distinct resemblance to the riots that broke out in the summer of 2020 in Minneapolis, Seattle, Portland, Chicago, New York, and other cities across the U. S. following the George Floyd incident: throwing bricks, looting shops, attacking the local cops, and setting bonfires in the streets. But Edgestow, unlike our contemporary American cities, had the N. I. C. E. police force directing hapless residents into the fray, instead of away from it.

In other words, the N. I. C. E. police were not breaking up the riot or stopping the looters; they were corralling residents into the riot areas so they would be victimized by the N. I. C. E. workmen (mercenary barbarians, to be more accurate), who were being well paid to destroy the local businesses and assault anyone who objected.

Fifty miles from the scene of the chaos, back at N. I. C. E. headquarters, Mark enjoys reading his own accounts of the riot in the morning papers as well as seeing the influence of his concocted news stories: "All agreed that the government would follow the most unanimous opinion of the nation (as expressed in the newspapers) and put it temporarily under control of the Institutional Police." But it isn't until the following day, when Mark decides to return to Edgestow, that he sees firsthand just how effective his articles have been at whitewashing the truth that the N. I. C. E. engineered the riot in order to vilify and push out the locals. At a pub just outside of town, Mark witnesses a long line of families carrying belongings on their backs: "These were the refugees from Edgestow. Some had been turned out of their houses, some scared by the riots and still more by the restoration of order. Something like a terror appeared to have been established in the town." Mark overhears some of the pub patrons describe what has happened, and what strikes him most deeply is their complete absence of indignation and their lack of sympathy for the refugees. Everyone at the pub knows of at least one outrage that has recently occurred in Edgestow, but all agree that these refugees must be greatly exaggerating their predicament: "It says in this morning's paper that things are pretty well settling down," relates the bartender, referring to one of Mark's own articles. The others respond that it's difficult to feel much sympathy for those residents since, as it says in the newspapers, they brought it all on themselves by engineering the riot. Clearly Mark's manufactured narrative has become, for them, reality.

A little later when Mark walks into Edgestow he finds the whole town wearing a new expression. One house out of three is empty. About half the shops have their windows boarded up. Many of these have been requisitioned and bear white placards with the N. I. C. E. symbol—a muscular male nude grasping a thunderbolt. At every street corner saunters the N. I. C. E. police—helmeted, swinging their clubs, with revolvers in holsters on their black, shiny belts. And "Emergency Regulations" notices are posted everywhere, bearing the signature of Lord Feverstone.

This is the turning point in Mark's life. Realizing what he's become as an institutional propagandist and how he's contributed to the destruction of the town and the livelihood of many of its residents, he attempts to leave the N. I. C. E. But the Left can be brutal even to its own, and one doesn't just leave an organization such as the N. I. C. E. with impunity. Every one of the Institute's manipulative tactics is now turned on him: He is framed for a murder he didn't commit; he is blackmailed, threatened, and psychologically abused with the intent to "recondition" him, much in the same way Big Brother's goons move to recondition Winston Smith in Orwell's *Nineteen Eighty-Four* (published, by the way, four years after Lewis's *That Hideous Strength*). In the dystopic vein of Orwell, Huxley, and Bradbury, Lewis's morality tale explores the perennial desire for man to enslave man by means of dehumanization. Unlike the other dystopian classics, however, *That Hideous Strength* is primarily satire, ridiculing academic politics, sham journalism, and the misuse of "science" just to name a few of his targets of criticism. And it works not only as satire for Lewis's original 20th-century postwar audience; it's eerily relevant as an indictment of aspects of our own age. Our information technology may have changed, but the propaganda techniques and the political desire to manipulate public opinion certainly have not. And, it is important to note, the desire to apply "science" to social engineering in order to achieve a stated improvement of society or to allegedly protect the well-being of the masses—in the utilitarian sense—resonates all too well. But Lewis, as a man and a scholar and a writer, is someone who understands what it means to be human. He recognizes—in this novel and in most of his other writings (*The Abolition of Man*, for example)—the perennial threats of dehumanization, including the misuse of science. Given the dubious "follow the science" narrative of 2020's COVID-19 response and recent developments in genetic engineering, psychopharmacology, and human cloning, there is, arguably, no greater subject for a cautionary tale in our own time than this.

PART THREE

Totalitarian Dreams

PROPAGANDA, MANIPULATION, & CONTROL

Nineteen Eighty-Four (1949)

GEORGE ORWELL

"Thoughtcrime does not entail death," writes Winston Smith, the protagonist of George Orwell's *Nineteen Eighty-Four*. "Thoughtcrime *is* death." Winston knows he is a dead man, but he's determined to stay alive as long as possible in an attempt to connect with like-minded rebels, who he isn't even sure exist. This one line penned in Winston's forbidden diary captures the essence of Orwell's Oceania, an oppressive society under a totalitarian government, technologically empowered to compel its citizens to think and act according to the dictates of English Socialism, known as Ingsoc.

Above all else, *Nineteen Eighty-Four* is a novel about social control, a control that depends wholly on the dehumanization of the individual in order to effect a collective orthodoxy, i.e., *the* proper way of thinking: a Party narrative made up of a countless number of "facts," even if patently untrue, to which all must enthusiastically assent—not simply in word and deed, but most importantly in thought. Even if those "facts" are fluid and may well change from week to week, and even from day to day, the individual must be willing to accept that narrative at any given point in time, even if it happens to contradict previously held beliefs promoted by Big Brother, the idol of the people and face of Party authoritarianism. The citizens of Oceania must not only jettison the principle of non-contradiction but actually convince themselves there is no contradiction and never was—a concept described in the novel as "doublethink." Those who even entertain a thought contrary to any jot or tittle of Oceanian orthodoxy are guilty of "thoughtcrime"—an unconscionable offense against the common good, one that is accorded an insufferable punishment beyond even Winston's wildest imagination. The net result: a citizenry not only stripped of human freedom and basic human rights but so dehumanized that each individual lacks any semblance of human dignity.

Not surprisingly, this control is effected by a pervasive fear that paralyzes the individual, preventing him from straying from the Party narrative and its expectations. Oceania is purposefully in a state of permanent stalemate war. Bombs drop indiscriminately on Winston's London twenty to thirty times each week, killing citizens almost daily, but the overwhelming implication is that these bombings are orchestrated by Oceania itself in order to keep its citizens in a perpetual state of fear and promote a blind patriotism to a government they are convinced will keep them safe. Not only are Oceania's citizens united against a common foreign enemy, but more importantly they are united against a common domestic threat in the form of "The Brotherhood," an invented shadow organization of saboteurs headed by the fictitious revolutionary Emmanuel Goldstein. As part of their daily work routine, Party members are expected to enthusiastically vilify Goldstein, the Brotherhood, and whichever superstate Oceania is currently at war with—according to the propaganda of the day. With all that time spent channeling hate, few find time to consider the authenticity of any of the Party's claims.

Yes, Winston Smith is Orwell's dystopian hero, "a lonely ghost uttering a truth that nobody would ever hear," as he prophetically acknowledges early on in his quixotic quest to rebel against the Party and its dehumanizing agenda. (It is worth noting that Orwell's original working title for the novel was *The Last Man in Europe*.) Winston's tragic flaw is a combination of curiosity—he is fascinated by the forbidden truth of the real past—and common sense abetted by a niggling nihilistic feeling that he's got nothing left to lose. Consequently, he ceases to operate out of fear, making him as dangerous as any man in Oceania, especially considering Winston himself is a Party bureaucrat working for the Records Department in the so-called Ministry of Truth. Winston's job is to, day by day and sometimes minute by minute, bring the past up to date. He "rectifies" historical records and newspaper articles to make them conform to Big Brother's most recent pronouncements, thus ensuring everything that the Party says remains "true." After "rectifying" some data about the chocolate ration, Winston hears of demonstrations to thank Big Brother for raising the chocolate ration to twenty grams a week. He reflects that on the previous day it had been announced that the ration was to be *reduced* to twenty grams a week. "Was it possible that they could swallow that, after only twenty-four hours?" asks Winston. "Yes, they swallowed it," and he knows that many swallowed it "fanatically, passionately, with a furious desire to track down, denounce, and vaporize anyone who should suggest that last week the ration had been thirty grams." Because Winston himself is a manufacturer of truth, he understands well the three primary means used by the Ministry of Truth to control the masses: the manipulation of language, the dependence on doublethink, and the mutability of the past.

One of Orwell's most enduring insights is the importance that language plays in shaping our thoughts and opinions. The government of Oceania understands this and carefully controls its citizens through the deceptive and manipulative use of language. Party orthodoxy is conditioned through the use of what we now call "information technology" and is policed by mass surveillance primarily through the use of the telescreen, a wall-sized, flat-screen display that can simultaneously send and receive audio and video. Every action is watched through centralized surveillance monitored by the Thought Police: "You had to live—did live, from habit that became instinct—in the assumption that every sound you made was overheard, and, except in darkness, every movement scrutinized." Winston, cognizant that even wearing an "improper expression" on one's face is itself a punishable offense, sets his features into "the expression of quiet optimism which it was advisable to wear when facing the telescreen."

Controlling one's language, of course, is every bit as difficult as controlling one's facial expressions, especially considering the citizens of Oceania are expected to rigorously abide by an enforced speech code known as Newspeak. First, the Party controls language by banning the use of content-rich words with multiple denotations; the stated Party goal is to eventually eliminate all words deemed complex enough to encourage nuanced or critical thought. Once this is accomplished, citizens are reduced to repeating meaningless slogans and regurgitating the latest "facts" they've heard on the telescreen, Oceania's equivalent of the mainstream media, relentlessly pumping out political propaganda aimed to further dehumanize its citizens by narrowing the range of thought.

Syme, one of Winston's colleagues at the Ministry of Truth, is working on the Eleventh Edition of the Newspeak dictionary. It's the "definitive edition," explains Syme with a pedant's passion. Syme doesn't invent new words; he destroys old ones: "scores of them, hundreds of them, every day. We're cutting the language down to the bone." And why? "In the end we shall make thoughtcrime literally impossible," Syme continues with vapid eagerness, "because there will be no words in which to express it. Every year fewer and fewer words, and the range of consciousness always a little smaller. The whole climate of thought will be different. In fact there will be no thought, as we understand it now. Orthodoxy means not thinking—not needing to think. Orthodoxy is unconsciousness." After all, an unthinking citizenry is what best serves an authoritarian state. Winston recalls his wife, who left him years before, as the Party's ideal unconscious no-nothing: "She had not a thought in her head that was not a slogan, and there was no imbecility, absolutely none, that she was not capable of swallowing if the Party handed it out to her."

Consequently, in Oceania, words are used not to convey meaning but to undermine it, corrupting the very ideas they refer to. Consider the "Ministry of Truth," both its name and its mission. Oceania is constantly bombarded with political propaganda broadcast all day long, made up of facts and figures, data which are primarily manufactured by the Ministry of Truth, and are sometimes, as with news of the chocolate ration, contradictory to previously manufactured truth. In today's world we disparagingly call this bald-face propaganda "fake news." Thus, in actual truth, the Ministry of Truth deals not with truth but with lies. In *Nineteen Eighty-Four,* "truth" is merely a manufactured item — what might more honestly be identified as carefully crafted lies. Thus, Winston and his colleagues in the Ministry of Truth are being asked to propagate disinformation while genuinely believing it. The rest of the citizenry is being asked to genuinely believe that which they know to be lies. This requires living in a state of cognitive dissonance in which one is compelled to disregard his own perception in place of the officially dictated version of events, leaving the individual completely dependent on the Party's version of reality. [Example: being told by a CNN anchor that "the protests are mostly peaceful" while standing in front of a burning building and an angry mob running by in the street.] In other words, the government enjoins its citizens to reject the evidence of their eyes and ears: "Life, if you looked about you, bore no resemblance not only to the lies that streamed out of the telescreens but even to the ideals that the Party was trying to achieve," Winston

observes. Consider the three-Party slogans on ubiquitous
public display: War Is Peace, Freedom Is Slavery, and Ignorance Is Strength. Each of these paradoxical expressions is
a contradiction in terms, especially considering Oceania is
at constant war, no one is free, and everyone is ignorant.
These slogans, although they each undermine the meaning
of the words they use, embody Party values. So, by the
manipulation of language, citizens come to believe that war,
slavery, and ignorance are values to be embraced as universal
goods. In order to intellectually accept these propositions,
this type of misuse of language requires the deliberate self-
deception known as "doublethink," a loyal willingness, in
contradiction to observed facts, to say, for example, that
black is white when the Party demands it. More importantly, it also means the ability *to believe* that black is white
and to forget that one has ever believed the contrary:

> To know and not to know, to be conscious of
> complete truthfulness while telling carefully con-
> structed lies, to hold simultaneously two opinions
> which canceled out, knowing them to be con-
> tradictory and believing in both of them, to use
> logic against logic, to repudiate morality while
> laying claim to it, to believe that democracy was
> impossible and that the Party was the guardian of
> democracy, to forget, whatever it was necessary to
> forget, then to draw it back into memory again
> at the moment when it was needed, and then
> promptly to forget it again.

Winston's job at the Ministry of Truth not only requires
him to assent to the paradoxical principle of doublethink;
it requires him to actively participate in the re-writing of
history. His position in the records department demands
that he destroy facts that have become inconvenient to
the Party, depositing them down "memory holes" that
lead to hidden furnaces beneath the building. He alters
previous news reports to conform with the running Party

narrative. He rewrites Big Brother's official speeches and pronouncements in such a way as to predict the thing that had actually happened. He rectifies original data by making them agree with later data, so that the Party can always claim it is and was correct. For example, after the Party issued its "categorical pledge" that there would be no reduction in the chocolate ration in the year 1984, it is Winston's job to rewrite that pledge as a warning that it would probably be necessary to reduce the ration sometime in April, when in fact the chocolate ration was reduced from thirty to twenty grams: "In this way every prediction made by the Party could be shown by documentary evidence to have been correct; nor was any item of news, or any expression of opinion, which conflicted with the needs of the moment, ever allowed to remain on record. All history was palimpsest, scraped clean and reinscribed exactly as often as was necessary." Others in the records department at the Ministry of Truth are charged with recalling and rewriting books, again and again, and those revised books are reissued without any admission that any alteration has been made. Another of Winston's colleagues is responsible, day after day, for tracking down and deleting from the press the names of people who have been "vaporized" on suspicion of thoughtcrimes against Party orthodoxy. They are deemed *unpersons*: "Your name was removed from the registers, every record of everything you had ever done was wiped out." It is as if the thoughtcrime perpetrator never existed—the ultimate indignity.

"Who controls the past, controls the future," runs a Party slogan that informs the mission of the Ministry of Truth, and "who controls the present controls the past." This mutability of the past, connected as it is with Newspeak and doublethink, might be the most important of Party maxims in Oceania's stratagem to maintain control over the individual. "The past," Winston reflects on his professional work, "had not merely been altered, it had been actually destroyed. For how could you establish even the most obvious fact when there existed no record outside your own memory?" With Winston's assistance, the past is erased, the erasure is forgotten, and the lie becomes truth. And since all records tell the same tale, the lie passes into history and becomes the accepted truth.

This Oceanian worldview is obviously influenced by the totalitarian regimes of the 20th century; Orwell admits he had Nazism and Stalin-era Soviet Communism in mind. But more importantly, Orwell is warning us of the potential for this occurring even in democratic societies. To be sure, language is being manipulated and the meaning of words undermined in the 21st century in order to control political thoughts and narrow the range of expression, terms are being redefined, euphemisms are in common use, and slogans are mindlessly repeated. A narrative of political correctness, if not the expectation of the State *per se*, is certainly promulgated through the telescreens of social media feeds and policed by the cultural ruling class, dominated by the media, the entertainment industry (music, sports, film, and television personalities), Big Tech, and campus intellectuals. Woe to he who in our day and age expresses a thought incongruous to the religion of "woke liberalism." He will be outed, publicly shamed, bullied, forced to apologize (often for a thoughtcrime he didn't even commit), and subsequently pledge his loyalty to the "woke" Party line—and even then he may still be ostracized or shunned for the rest of his professional career. New Orleans Saints quarterback Drew Brees provides a case in point. In June of 2020, Brees voiced his displeasure with athletes who kneel before the American flag during the National Anthem. "I will never agree with anybody disrespecting the flag of the United States of America," said Brees in a livestreamed interview with Yahoo! Finance (June 3, 2020). He explained that when he sees the American flag he thinks of his two grandfathers who fought for the country during World War II, risking their lives to protect their country. "So every time I stand with my hand over my heart, looking at that flag and singing the national anthem, that's what I think about," he added. For these brief comments, Brees was attacked by a woke Twitter mob, led by the formidable LeBron James. The basketball legend excoriated Brees for his lack of understanding of woke orthodoxy. Kneeling during the National anthem, @ KingJames tweeted, "has nothing to do with disrespect for the flag or our soldiers who keep our land free." Richard Sherman piled on, tweeting that Brees "is beyond lost," criticizing him for conflating kneeling during the anthem with disrespect for the military. Brees however was objecting to the conflation of police brutality and racism with the American flag, something the Twitter mob seems not to understand. The meaning of the American flag (and the National Anthem, too), they are arguing, does not represent fighting for freedom and a respect for the military defense of the country. The problem here for Brees is that the woke mob redefined the meaning of the flag and the anthem, just as Oceania's propagandists redefine terms to suit Big Brother's orthodox narrative. The 41-year-old former MVP fell afoul of woke orthodoxy because he did not realize that. After being bullied by fellow athletes, including members of his own team—those who *know* Brees is no racist and conveniently disregard the fact—Brees was publicly humiliated and forced to apologize. "I would like to apologize to my friends, teammates, the city of New Orleans, the black community, the NFL community, and anyone I hurt with my comments yesterday," he said in a statement on social media the very next day. "In speaking with some of you, it breaks my heart to know the pain I have caused. In an attempt to talk about respect, unity, and solidarity centered around the American flag and the national anthem, I made comments that were insensitive and completely missed the mark on issues we are facing right now as a country."

Brees added that he was "sick about the way my comments were perceived, but I take full responsibility." He followed that abject apology by repeating the slogans he is expected to believe about "systemic racial injustice" and "police brutality" in an attempt to expiate his "sin" against woke orthodoxy. If he didn't buy into this plank of the woke platform before, he quickly assented to the narrative that the police in the U. S. (despite statistics to the contrary) wake up each day itching to murder black men in the line of duty. It is instructive to note that despite his apology, Brees was still accused of not understanding the issue and not doing enough. "The apology felt late. Not just a day late. Four years late," wrote Ann Killion in the *San Francisco Chronicle* (June 5, 2020), who accused the "high profile white athlete" of being silent for the previous four years since San Francisco's quarterback Colin Kaepernick introduced the practice of kneeling during the National Anthem in protest of police brutality against black Americans. This is the same Drew Brees who helped Hurricane Katrina victims rebuild playgrounds and parks in predominantly African-American neighborhoods. This is the same Drew Brees who donated five million dollars to feed the hungry during the coronavirus pandemic which hit the African-American neighborhoods of New Orleans particularly hard. (Nancy Armour, in a June 5, 2020, opinion piece in *USA Today*, wrote that Brees should "make another donation, this time to researchers studying the harmful impact systemic racism has on the health of people of color, given that African-Americans are twice as likely to die of COVID-19.") This is the same Drew Brees who established mentor programs for inner-city children in predominantly African-American neighborhoods. Yet, despite the fact that Brees stands firmly in solidarity with black Americans, he is accused of thoughtcrime, humiliated, and professionally executed even after apologizing. In fact, it is safe to say that Brees has done more for black Americans than the vast majority of his vociferous critics, a fact that is conveniently lost in the kerfuffle simply because Brees dared to color outside the lines of woke orthodoxy.

In contrast to Drew Brees, who actually said something with which others could disagree, Aleksandar Katai was summarily fired by Major League Soccer's Los Angeles Galaxy for comments his wife made (in Serbian) on social media—unbeknownst to Katai. In the days following the police-involved death of George Floyd, Katai's wife referred to the rioters, looters, and arsonists in Minneapolis as "disgusting cattle." This comment was, rightly or wrongly, construed by the LA Galaxy and the much of the Twitterverse as aimed at African-Americans and deemed racist, even though video footage clearly reveals that plenty of the rioters were white, like Katai. Nonetheless, the LA Galaxy strongly condemned Tea Katai's social media posts and requested their immediate removal. The team said in a statement: "The LA Galaxy stands firmly against racism of any kind, including that which suggests violence or seems to demean the efforts of those in pursuit of racial equality." Even though Alexsandar Katai made no racially biased comments himself (nor did his wife, it can be argued), he made a public apology, stating, "I strongly condemn white supremacy, racism and violence towards people of color. Black lives matter. This is a mistake from my family and I take full responsibility. I will ensure that my family and I take the necessary actions to learn, understand, listen and support the black community." The next day Katai was fired anyway and professionally executed, given that it is unlikely that any other MLS team will ever again sign him to play.

Winston Smith's path takes a similar trajectory but with consequences far more dire. Though Winston is intelligent enough to see through Party propaganda, he is no match for co-worker O'Brien, a member of the elite Inner Party two percent, whom Winston mistakes as a clandestine saboteur working for the elusive (and fictional, it turns out)

Brotherhood. O'Brien lures Winston into his lair, posing as one of Emmanuel Goldstein's lieutenants of resistance only to trap him into admissions of unorthodoxy that get him arrested. It turns out that O'Brien himself is a high-ranking member of the Thought Police. And it is through O'Brien that Orwell discloses the authoritarian animus for complete control of the individual. "The Party seeks power entirely for its own sake," he admits. "We know that no one ever seizes power with the intention of relinquishing it. Power is not a means, it is an end." The ultimate aim of the Party, says O'Brien, is to gain and retain full power over all the people of Oceania—every individual person, without exception: "If you want a picture of the future, imagine a boot stamping on a human face—forever."

What happens to Winston in the end can be compared to that boot stamping on a human face. He is tortured by O'Brien in the Ministry of Love as a part of the "re-education" process to "cure" him of his hatred for the Party. The purpose of the torture is not to extract a fake confession, but to actually alter what Winston thinks. Early in the novel, Winston writes in his diary, *"Freedom is the freedom to say that two plus two make four. If that is granted, all else follows."* Winston is traumatized into complete intellectual surrender. In the end, he is not only willing to say two plus two make five, but by all appearances he actually believes it. Once his soul is crushed and the Party has sufficiently dehumanized him, Winston Smith is deemed ready to be re-introduced into society, docile and obedient and without moral purpose. As if that's not bad enough, the final words of the novel are perhaps the most chilling of all: "He had won the victory over himself. He loved Big Brother." In effect, O'Brien's boot was stamping on Winston's face, and it would remain there forever.

"Politics and the English Language" (1946)

GEORGE ORWELL

*J*n his 1946 essay "Politics and the English Language," George Orwell poses a thoughtful question: Is language "a natural growth" or is it shaped "for our own purposes"? In other words, does the English language organically evolve over time or is it purposefully manipulated in order to affect the social order? Anyone familiar with Orwell's *Nineteen Eighty-Four* can probably guess at the trajectory of his response. Although one could argue that this seminal essay on 20th-century linguistics was written merely to lament the "general collapse" of language as a reflection of the general collapse of civilization following the Second World War, Orwell's ultimate purpose is to show that socio-political agendas can unduly manipulate language to their own ends by obscuring meaning, corrupting thought, and rendering language a minefield in the political landscape. And why? Orwell says: to effect changes in thought and affections and to shame those who somehow prove impervious to manipulation.

Orwell dramatizes this assertion in *Nineteen-Eighty-Four*. Published three years after his "Politics and the English Language," the iconic dystopic novel imagines a futuristic government that manipulates language so that its citizens conform in thought, word, and deed to its narrow political orthodoxy. Language, in fact, is the primary change agent, assisted by government-engineered fearmongering and savage punishments reserved for language dissidents.

Just as language matters in the world of *Nineteen-Eighty-Four*, it matters in our world too. Consider, for example, the basics of inclusive language. Back when Orwell was writing and throughout much of the 20th century, the accepted universal singular pronouns were *he/him/his*, a reality codified in every English grammar text published before 1999. In other words, these pronouns were used to refer to any individual, whether male or female, as in, "Every student should bring his book to class." The meaning was clear, the convention was understood, and because it was an accepted grammatical convention, no one was denounced as sexist for applying its usage. Some years later, in an effort to be inclusive, language handlers in academia and the publishing industry pointed out that the convention itself was sexist and reinforced sexism in society. If they could change the convention, they reasoned, they could change society.

The language handlers first promoted the alternative "inclusive" usage of *he or she / him or her / his or hers*—and then soon thereafter demanded it. Those, especially men, who continued using traditional grammatical constructions that included the universal pronouns *he/him/his* were singled out for particularly harsh treatment, often branded—on the basis of their grammar alone—as sexists. But mere social stigma—*you, boy, are a male chauvinist pig*—later gave way to punitive actions. For example, in 2013, California State University (Chico) revised their definition of sexual harassment and sexual violence to include "continual use of generic masculine terms such as to refer to people of both sexes." Thus, Chico profs who say, "Every student should bring his book to class" are liable to punitive actions, up to and including dismissal. As you might imagine, Chico is not alone in this. Rather, this is the norm on most college campuses.

But now, in 2020, it is apparently no longer acceptable to use "he or she" or "him or her." What was once promoted and then demanded by language handlers as inclusive has now been deemed *verboten* by the same people! Who are these language handlers? In brief, they are the engineers of the English language style manuals used by academia, the media, and the publishing industry, all easy prey to special interest lobbyists who demand language changes to promote their socio-political agendas. Last year, for example, the American Psychological Association (APA) announced a change to its stylebook, advocating for the singular "they" because it is "inclusive of all people and helps writers avoid making assumptions about gender." The APA style guide makes it clear that the usage of "his or her" is no longer inclusive and no longer acceptable. This could not have happened without the proponents of transgenderism pushing for manipulation of language. In order for the APA's statement to make any sense—"They... is inclusive of all people and helps writers avoid making assumptions about gender"—one is forced to accept the premises of transgenderism including the theory of so-called nonbinary gender. If one is to properly accept the usage of the singular *they*, one must also accept the fantasy that an infinite number of genders exists and that language is tied to something called "gender expression" rather than to sex, which is binary: male and female.

In 2018, the National Council of Teachers of English (NCTE) released a "Statement on Gender and Language" promoting the use of the singular *they* as the only inclusive universal pronoun. In its position statement, the NCTE actually spells out the premises one must accept in order to logically make sense of the singular *they*. This is not about language clarity or precision; this is about advancing a socio-political agenda that requires everyone—yes, everyone—to accept the following terms:

- *Gender identity*: an individual's feeling about, relationship with, and understanding of gender as it pertains to their sense of self. An individual's gender identity may or may not be related to the sex that individual was assigned at birth.
- *Gender expression*: external presentation of one's gender identity, often through behavior, clothing, haircut, or voice, which may or may not conform to socially defined behaviors and characteristics typically associated with being either masculine or feminine.
- *Cisgender*: of or relating to a person whose gender identity corresponds with the sex they were assigned at birth.
- *Transgender*: of or relating to a person whose gender identity differs from the sex they were assigned at birth. This umbrella term may refer to someone whose gender identity is woman or man, or to someone whose gender identity is nonbinary (see below).
- *Nonbinary*: of or relating to a person who does not identify, or identify solely, as either a woman or a man. More specific nonbinary identifiers include but are not limited to terms such as agender and gender fluid (see below).
- *Gender fluid*: of or relating to individuals whose identity shifts among genders. This term overlaps with terms such as genderqueer and bigender, implying movement among gender identities and/or presentations.
- *Agender*: of or relating to a person who does not identify with any gender, or who identifies as neutral or genderless.

The NCTE, like the APA, the *Chicago Manual of Style* (CMS), and the *Associated Press* (AP), not only advocates using the singular *they*, it also prohibits "using *he* as a universal pronoun" and "using binary alternatives such as *he/she, he or she*, or *(s)he*." And, in case you don't understand the prohibition, the NCTE provides an example of the forbidden "exclusionary (binary)" language: "Every cast member should know *his or her* lines by Friday" must be written as "Every cast member should know *their* lines by Friday." The proper convention presents an offense against the dignity of traditional grammar usage since the plural pronoun, *their,* does not agree with its singular subject, *member.* (Really now, wouldn't a simple re-write render the sentence both grammatically correct and "inclusive": *All cast members should know their lines by Friday.*) And, also according to NCTE, in the case of a student named Alex, who declares that his preferred pronouns are *they/them/their,* a teacher should say, "Alex needs to learn their lines by Friday." Yes, seriously, this is the example given by the NCTE. (And whose lines, one may ask? Everyone's lines? It's just so lacking in precision and clarity, and this from the organization that exerts enormous influence over our nation's high school English teachers.) To be sure, these teachers and their students will be forced to pronounce the ridiculous: *Alex needs to learn their lines by Friday.* Failing to do so could, in the near future, be construed as gender harassment and be cause for expulsion or sacking.

So, why does it matter what the APA or the *Chicago Manual of Style* or the NCTE has to say on the matter of nonbinary gender-inclusive language and the singular *they*? Well, the APA sets the writing style and format conventions for academic essays for many college and high school students as well as for scholarly articles and books. The *Chicago Manual of Style* (published by the University of Chicago) sets the editorial standards and conventions widely used in the publishing industry. And the NCTE, as mentioned previously, sets the tone for high school English teachers across the nation, those who will teach our children to read, write, and speak.

In "Politics and the English Language," Orwell calls this "an invasion of one's mind"—again, the purposeful manipulation of language in order to corrupt one's thoughts and affections. Thus, the choice of academia, the media, and the publishing industry to adopt the singular *they* usage is not simply about word choice—as silly and illogical as it may be: *Alex needs to learn their lines by Friday!*—it is about forcing students and others to accept the language of transgenderism and the ideological corollaries behind the vocabulary. It is asking us all to accept something that is less than reality. Pronouns, we are told, are no longer related to the body (male and female) but to the mind, how one "identifies" or "expresses" the social construct of gender. The reality is denied, and the fluid world of one's nonbinary fancy replaces it.

It is worth noting that last year the Vatican's Congregation for Catholic Education published a 30-page document on this very topic. Quoting Pope Francis, "Male and Female He Created Them" explains that gender theory "denies the difference and reciprocity in nature of a man and a woman and envisages a society without sexual differences, thereby eliminating the anthropological basis of the family." This ideology, Pope Francis explains, promotes "a personal identity and emotional intimacy radically separated from the biological difference between male and female. Consequently, human identity becomes the choice of the individual, one which can also change over time." Thus, in the case of the Catholic educator or the Catholic student, one must compromise his religious principles in order to conform to the industry standards of language.

This attempt to transplant pronouns from the body to the mind, Orwell might say, is an attempt to destroy our ability to communicate. According to this new norm, one can now choose from a multitude of "gender identities"—or simply make up a new one—none of which has any fixed link to a specific set of pronouns. (Some recently emerging gender pronouns include: *zir, ze, xe, hir, per, ve, ey, hen, thon*. And there are more! Facebook, for example, offers 50 options. Fifty!) In fact, following this reasoning, gender expressionists may, at any time and for any reason, decide to change their preferred personal pronouns but without changing their gender identity; they may also decide to change their gender identity without changing their preferred pronouns—or they may choose to change both. This is the kind of linguistic pretention that, as Orwell warns, obscures meaning, corrupts thought, and renders language a minefield in the political landscape. Why a minefield? As Orwell illustrated with *Nineteen-Eighty-Four*, precisely because part and parcel of language engineering is attempting to shame or punish those who disagree with the ascribed linguistic orthodoxy. And, again, to what end? As Chicago-based community activist Saul Alinsky famously wrote in his manifesto "Rules for Radicals": "He who controls the language controls the masses." (Note his use of "sexist language" by way of the universal singular pronoun *he*.) Alinsky, an enthusiastic advocate of manipulating language for political purposes, agrees with Orwell: It's all about thought control; it's about superimposing a socio-political ideology on the masses; it's about altering our understanding of the world; it's about customizing the language to effect whimsical social change. It's ultimately about altering reality so that, as Orwell dramatized in *Nineteen-Eighty-Four*, we come to accept that "war is peace," that "freedom is slavery," and that two plus two equals five.

Orwell, as evidenced by his "Politics and the English Language," believes that language should reflect reality. If it doesn't, what possible limits could ever be placed on misleading, manipulative language, whether in grade school textbooks, government documents, or political campaign literature? If language is "always evolving," as many commentators have reasoned in their recent support of so-called nonbinary gender-inclusive language (including the "singular *they*"), what is stopping anyone from using this as an excuse to effect any change in any language for any reason at any time?

Fahrenheit 451 (1953)

RAY BRADBURY

*G*reat literature teaches us about ourselves. Dystopian literature warns us of who we might become. In Ray Bradbury's *Fahrenheit 451*, we recognize who we've been and what we've become over the past seven decades. We didn't heed Bradbury's warning; we merely fulfilled his prophecy. Not only did he accurately predict back in 1953 the pervasive use of 21st-century technologies that tend to detach us from reality and alienate us from one another—iPods and earbuds, "screen time" and binge-watching—he also predicted the unfortunate results of progressive educational trends and the dominance of an entertainment culture that separates us from our moral purpose. Bradbury's dystopia is a secular society that breaks with the cultural and historical past, disregards the wisdom of the ages, and criminalizes the possession of books—*all* books—because they may cause readers to question the status quo and consequently present a threat to the political stability of their soft tyranny.

The novel takes its name from the temperature at which paper burns. The iconic gimmick of *Fahrenheit 451* is the profession of the fireman, who no longer puts out fires but starts them. (Bradbury did not predict the rise of a political correctness that would necessitate these public servants being called *firefighters*.) These state-sanctioned arsonists carry out their duty to protect society not from the consuming flames of fire but from the malicious impact of books and their potential grand messages. Guy Montag is one such fireman, one whom Bradbury uses as his tragic protagonist, one whom we recognize in all effective dystopian novels: the character who begins to question the status quo, later becomes a rebel, and then is hunted as a rogue.

It is through Montag's wife Mildred, however, that Bradbury demonstrates the sicknesses of his imagined society. He uses her character and her interactions with Montag to illustrate the typical citizen, detached and alienated, amused yet depressed. Mildred spends most of her waking hours immersed in an escapist virtual reality, binge-watching television on her giant flat-screen TVs that take up the entirety of three walls of her living room. The characters in her favorite "shows" have so much become her family that she refers to them as her TV aunts and uncles. She even believes that she herself has become a character in these shows—a sort of Hollywood niece.

When not enjoying her television aunts and uncles, Mildred sports what we would now call earbuds or AirPods, even when in conversation with her husband: "In her ears the little Seashells, the thimble radios tamped tight and an electric ocean of sound, of music and talk, music and talk, coming in on the shore of her unsleeping mind." Of course, with streaming music and talk perpetually pumped into her ears, she's unable to have a meaningful conversation. In fact, she really has nothing to talk about. Not even her television shows. When pressed by Montag to explain what's going on in an episode playing loudly in the background, she gives only a vague response. Clearly unaware of any plot or conflict, she is immersed in vacuity, the nothingness of television, which serves her as some fleeting pleasure that provides a distraction from real life. "It's really fun," Mildred tells Montag with a straight face. "It'll be even more fun when we can afford to have the fourth wall installed."

For Mildred, this lifestyle of constant distraction is an addiction, one that includes ending each day with sleeping pills to send her off to la-la land. One night, after returning home from burning down an old man's house, Montag finds Mildred, as usual, "stretched on the bed, uncovered and cold, like a body displayed on the lid of a tomb, her eyes fixed to the ceiling by invisible threads of steel, immovable." On this occasion, after discovering an empty bottle of sleeping tablets "which earlier today had been filled with thirty capsules and which now lay uncapped and empty," Montag phones the "emergency hospital," which sends over two "operators" with a roto-rooter-like contraption to pump her stomach and clean her blood while they stand over her nonchalantly smoking. Like plumbers working to unclog the pipes, they quickly finish their routine and head off with a case of Mildred's "liquid melancholy." When Montag asks why the hospital didn't send a doctor, one of the operators explains, "We get these cases nine or ten a night. Got so many, starting a few years ago, we had the special machines built. You don't need an M. D., case like this, all you need is two handymen, clean up the problem in half an hour." In the morning, Montag wakes to find Mildred making toast, complaining of being very hungry but having no recollection of the sleeping pills, the handymen, or the "cleaning" she received. Clearly Mildred's case is not unique. "Nobody knows anyone," Montag laments. "Strangers come and violate you. Strangers come and cut your heart out. Strangers come and take your blood out. Good God, who *were* those men?"

Clarisse McClellan is the real star of this dystopian tale, despite the fact that she goes missing and is presumed dead by page 32, likely mowed down by a fast-driving road-rager. Clarisse is Montag's seventeen-year-old neighbor who recently moved into the neighborhood. When he sees her out in her yard knitting a sweater or shaking chestnuts from a tree, she happily chats him up, asking him questions about what he does as a firemen, getting him to examine his unexamined life. While people like Mildred are lost in their television shows and sleeping pills, Clarisse takes an authentic interest in the world around her, both nature and other people. "I rarely watch the 'parlor walls' or go to the races or Fun Parks," she happily explains. And then she expounds on how much greater it is to be a pedestrian than a driver, how she and her family love to sit around at home and talk and laugh and enjoy one another's company. Not only is Clarisse young and beautiful and radiant, she is the only citizen in this society who still seems to know what it means to be human, who values human relationships, and believes in being social. The irony is that Clarisse McClellan is sent to see a psychiatrist for what her school considers being "anti-social." The psychiatrist, she says, "wants to know why I go out and hike around the forest and watch the birds and collect the butterflies." School officials wonder how she can just walk around thinking about the world. They are confounded by her objections to their model of schooling: getting students together to watch televised indoctrination sessions and play sports, all the while being forbidden from talking to anyone. This schooling, she says, is what's anti-social, not her.

Clarisse McClellan is clearly the inciting force that gets Montag thinking about the absurdity of his re-purposed profession. In one exchange, Clarisse tells Montag that she isn't afraid of him: "So many people are. Afraid of firemen, I mean. But you're just a man after all." She knows very well what he does for a living and gently challenges him with one simple question that sets the rest of the story in motion: "Are you happy?"

We see Montag and his fireman colleagues in action in one particularly illustrative scene in which an old woman refuses to leave her home once the professional arsonists break down her door with the brass nozzles of kerosene hoses in hand to incinerate her secret book collection: "They were up in musty blackness swinging silver hatchets at doors that were, after all, unlocked, tumbling through like boys all rollick and shout." This modus operandi takes its cues from Gestapo tactics. The home invasions always happen at night, the homeowner is always taken by surprise, and the enforcers have invariably been tipped off by some well-meaning snitch of a neighbor convinced he's doing his civic duty. Instead of searching for Jews hidden in closets and secret compartments, the firemen hunt down the secret stash of books like a predator sniffing out its prey. As routine practice would have it in Bradbury's imagined future world, the firemen don't just blacken the books; they set the whole house alight and watch it burn to the ground. In this case, since the old woman refuses to leave her library, she's burned to death together with her books.

As brutal and as memorable as this scene may be, the primary problem with books in this society is not that they get burned. The primary problem is that precious few people have any interest in reading them. Through a *Brave New World*-style social conditioning, the citizens of Bradbury's dystopia are convinced that books contain trivial nothingness at best and revolutionary lies at worst. "You know the law," scolds Captain Beatty when he discovers the old lady's stash, accusing her of being a brainwashed old fool. "You've been locked up here for years with a regular damn Tower of Babel. Snap out of it! The people in those books never lived. Come on now!"

Of course Captain Beatty has it wrong. It's not the old woman who's been brainwashed. It's everyone else. They've all been conditioned through schooling and political messaging to believe that the whole idea of literature is superfluous and repulsive. Books aren't vessels of meaning or carriers of culture, students are taught. They are meaningless diversions from the life of amusement and pleasure they are expected to lead. After all, why bother with books when you can be entertained by vacuous television sitcoms or get your news in informational soundbites, 24 hours a day?

Montag, inspired by Clarisse to ask questions about the status quo, begins by wondering about books. "There must be something in books," he says to the unsympathetic Mildred, "things we can't imagine, to make a woman stay in a burning house; there must be something there. You don't stay for nothing." Once it becomes obvious that Montag has a morbid curiosity about books and questions why his sole professional purpose is to rid the world of them, Captain Beatty makes a house-call to explain the company line. Film and radio, he says, began the streamlining process that eventually made books superfluous to education and entertainment. At first, books were cut shorter: "Condensations. Digests. Tabloids." And then, Beatty continues, "Classics cut to fit fifteen-minute radio shows, then cut again to fill a two-minute book column, winding up at last as a ten- or twelve-line dictionary resume." People's only knowledge of Shakespeare's *Hamlet,* for example, comes from "a one-page digest." Meaning and depth—and therefore the intellectual and emotional impact—have been jettisoned in favor of easily digestible nuggets of info that offer the impression of knowledge, reminding one of social media news feeds with titillating and often misleading headlines that form a running narrative for us. Although Beatty's explanation of the devolution of literature parallels the reality of what we've witnessed in our own world over the past seventy years, it doesn't go a long way to satisfying Montag's curiosity about why his professional life is devoted to "burning books to ash, and then burning the ashes."

Like Huxley's Bernard Marx and Orwell's Winston Smith, Guy Montag's big mistake is to begin to think for himself, to ask questions, especially about those aspects of society that defy reason. For Montag, the questions do begin with books, but he eventually realizes that the suppression of books and the ideas contained within them is merely an indication of a greater universal problem: People have ceased to be fully human. Like Mildred, whose life is spent passively entertaining herself, devoid of any meaningful human relationships, few in Bradbury's dystopian future are living their lives with a moral purpose. These are a people whose intellect, emotions, and creativity have been enslaved to a pervasive mindlessness that ultimately serves the invisible overlords of big government. There is no reason, no meaning, and no purpose to life. There's only pleasure and amusement.

Bradbury reminds us that fleeting pleasure can be gained from a variety of activities: watching the aunts and uncles of the parlor walls, listening to streaming podcasts, driving at 100 mph. Lasting happiness, however, can only be achieved through cultivation of soul and mind, which requires us to live with a moral purpose. Only Clarisse McClellan seems to understand this concept, connected as it is to the natural world around her. It is she who opens Montag's eyes to this world—the smell of the flowers, the look of the moon, the taste of raindrops, the blowing of a leaf across the sidewalk, the value of meaningful conversation. What makes human beings unique is our capacity to reason and to use that reason to investigate the nature of the world and our purpose in it. This is precisely what the citizens of *Fahrenheit 451* are not doing. With few exceptions, like a Clarisse McClellan, they are living with no moral purpose. Any communal moral purpose has been eradicated with the burning of books, whose collective ideas once formed the basis of culture and a successful civilization. These citizens have no understanding of a God who loves them, no understanding that they are all made in the image and likeness of God, endowed with rights and duties. Without any individual moral purpose, these people are doomed to live unexamined lives of amoral hedonism, moving from one fleeting pleasure to the next—anything to prevent meaningful conversation or thought—until they drop dead and have their bodies cremated: "Ten minutes after death a man's a speck of black dust," explains Captain Beatty. "Let's not quibble over individuals with memoriums. Forget them. Burn all. Burn everything." This is secular nihilism at its lowest.

After Montag turns from rebel to rogue, armed with a copy of the Holy Bible, he goes off the grid to join the resistance—a group of men who commit to memory the contents of important books so that they themselves will become, reverting to the oral tradition, living carriers of culture. Bradbury, staying on script, treats Montag as the classic dystopian hero, who like Hamlet is brought low by his own heroics. After all, if these rogues are becoming the new books, we shouldn't be surprised if they become the new "objects" of vengeful conflagration. Captain Beatty's words echo, "Burn all. Burn everything."

So what was Bradbury's warning to us back in 1953? Even before every American household had a television, he foresaw the deleterious effects of a pervasive entertainment culture. If we continue to cede our lives to Hollywood and the technology that brings it to us, he warned, we will fall prey to consumerism and become a vacuous people concerned with little more than our own amusements. People will jettison God and neighbor in favor of binge-watching their "favorite shows," scrolling through social media feeds, living vicariously through sports figures and video games, and taking vacations from reality by the use of prescription drugs. Bradbury warned that we risk becoming Mildred, that without moral purpose we risk ceasing to be fully human.

The Thanatos Syndrome (1987)

WALKER PERCY

When Walker Percy was 29 years old, the agnostic Southern physician converted to Catholicism and left medicine to became a novelist. Even back in the 1940s he had become increasingly disconcerted by the American reliance on science to solve all human problems. Percy was particularly disturbed by the narrow way the medical field described illness—a problem is named; treatment is prescribed—and the increasing reliance on pharmaceutical companies to provide pill-popping solutions to psychological problems. It bothered him that people were being treated like broken machines rather than flawed human beings, and he came quickly to understand that the more we place our trust in science to solve our human problems, the more alienated we become from ourselves and from our community. The ultimate problem, he discovered, is not medical but existential. In 1966 he wrote: "What began to interest me was not the physiological and pathological processes within man's body but the problem of man himself, the nature and destiny of man; specifically and more immediately, the predicament of man in a modern technological society." He described this predicament as feeling "lost in the cosmos," the title of his 1983 mock self-help manual. This alienation as he understood it stemmed in part from the pervasive belief that natural science has the truth—*all* the truth, that something can be called "truth" only when it can be verified by the scientific method.

Percy, however, appreciated that science cannot account for the whole range of human experience—emotions, art, and faith, for starters. He realized that it could neither account for the meaning of individual lives nor for a common morality. So, he turned to writing in order to explore the meaning of life. Each of his novels features an upper middle-class male protagonist who is in one way or another "lost in the cosmos." In his sixth and final novel, *The Thanatos Syndrome* (1987), Tom More is Percy's thinly veiled *alter ego*, a disgraced psychiatrist in the throes of just such an existential crisis. Like his canonized 16th-century English counterpart, Tom is an iconoclast. In this sequel to *Love in the Ruins* (1971), Percy follows in the footsteps of Aldous Huxley to explore what happens when scientific solutions are writ large—when these scientific solutions become the primary way to solve the problems of society rather than to help individual persons.

When Tom returns to his hometown practice in Louisiana after serving a two-year sentence in a minimum security prison for selling amphetamines at a truck stop, he notices bizarre behavioral changes in his former patients. "In each there has occurred a sloughing away of the old terrors, worries, rages, a shedding of guilt like last year's snakeskin, and in its place is a mild fond vacancy, a species of unfocused animal good spirits," he observes. His patients' mental and emotional problems seem to have been "fixed" in his absence but their personalities radically transformed. They have stopped acting like themselves and more like one another, mild-mannered and compliant. Their verbal communication skills are wanting and they use language out of context without reference to themselves, but they are also mysteriously gifted with impeccable recall and the ability to solve complex mathematical equations without a calculator—the sort of skills and characteristics that together would make one a formidable but quirky poker player with an unflinching, stoic face. How, Tom wonders, have these

people become so robotic and unemotional, even as they
no longer suffer from panic attacks, depression, anxiety,
or OCD? Less apparent at first blush is the near total loss
of individuality, and therefore the dignity, of the human
person. This is how Percy sets the stage for a showdown
between love of the individual and abstract compassion for
humanity. Percy dramatizes what might happen to society
if all personal struggles are defined as medical problems to
be solved by the pharmaceutical industry and their acolytes,
solved not for the good of the individual, but for the alleged
benefit of society. Tom soon understands it's not just his
patients who are exhibiting these odd behavioral changes,
it's almost all the residents of his hometown in Feliciana
parish, including his own estranged wife and children.

Because Dr. Tom More has been disgraced in his profession, he comes under the influence of Bob Comeaux,
a former colleague who makes Tom "an offer you can't
refuse." Good old avuncular Bob is a DC-indoctrinated
fed, director of the Quality-of-Life Division of the Fed-
eral Complex overseeing euthanasia programs. (Not to
go unnoticed: This is what Walker Percy envisioned for
the future of American medicine, a kind of advanced
Dutch system where the practices of killing of infants
up to eighteen months old and killing of the elderly are
carried out under government supervision. In other words,
public health officials on the advice of medical experts
can determine whether an unwanted or diseased life is
worthwhile, whether an unborn baby should be aborted, or
whether an ill person should go on living.) Bob Comeaux
is going to make Tom's probationary problems disappear,
appoint him senior consultant on the Nuclear Regulatory
Commission's Advisory Committee for the Medical Use of
Isotopes, pay him a modest salary, and provide him with
an office and lab space to do his own research.

But there's a catch. Tom, described by Bob Comeaux as
knowing "more about the brain pharmacology of isotopes

than anyone else," must become complicit in his hush-hush social engineering program call Project Blue Boy. Yes, the feds are blackmailing Tom. The unspoken corollary of Bob's "offer you can't refuse" is this: If you don't join us, we will help you find your way back to prison. Tom's unique medical expertise is needed, Bob assures him, and he'll be putting that expertise to work at the service of humanity, curing all manner of social problems that plague the world today. "What would you say if I gave you a magic wand," Bob asks, "and Tom could cure all manner of social ills overnight?"

Project Blue Boy, that magic wand to "improve" society, involves secretly dumping heavy sodium into the water supply. As a result, violent crime decreases and teenage pregnancy drops; child abuse and wife-beating become rare; hospital admissions for depression, chemical dependence, and anxiety are reduced by seventy-nine percent. On top of all that, boasts Bob, "these same subjects have an average twenty percent increase in I. Q.—plus an almost total memory recall which makes you and me look like dummies." Tom understands that, out of context, all of this sounds unequivocally beneficial to everyone involved and makes for great news-bite statistics for politicians racing to take credit for waning social ills. However, having witnessed the behavior of those who are presumably the "beneficiaries" of this social engineering, Tom also knows that they have all lost the distinctiveness of their personalities, they answer questions like automatons, they have ceased to be individuals.

Tainting the water supply with heavy sodium, as it is explained in the novel, controls behavior by altering the brain's neurochemistry: "We know that the heavy ion inhibits dopamine production in the prefrontal cortex," explains Bob, "which as you know is probably the chemical basis of schizophrenia. We know it increases endorphin production, which as you know gives you a drug-free natural high." In its purpose, the tainted water supply is reminiscent of *Brave New World's* wonder drug "soma," conceived as an expedient way to control the behavior of the masses so as not to upset the totalitarian political order. It is instructive to note here that *The Thanatos Syndrome* was published the same year the highly touted antidepressant Prozac was introduced. Thus, Percy was writing before the so-called Prozac wars, the ongoing debates about the efficacy and safety of powerful mood-altering drugs. Obviously, Percy was familiar with the moral and ethical implications of using psychopharmacology to alter one's mood and personality, never mind all the unintended consequences.

But Tom identifies an even more pressing moral concern. When Bob challenges him to "name one thing we're doing wrong," Tom says he sees an obvious civil rights abuse: "You're assaulting the cortex of an individual without the knowledge or consent of the assaultee." But Bob Comeaux dismisses Tom's concerns, likening Project Blue Boy to the fluoridation of the water supply fifty years before. It was done for the good of society, he says. And if it promotes public health, why should we need consent from individuals?

That statement perhaps more than any other demonstrates the essential differences in the moral and ethical world views of Bob Comeaux and Tom More vis-à-vis the use and promises of science. Bob believes that every social ill can be effectively combatted by some scientific advancement, that every aberration in human behavior can be explained by something in the brain that can be "fixed" by psychopharmacology. Although he says his goal is to help humanity by alleviating human suffering, he is incapable of loving or caring for the individual person, incapable of understanding the importance of individuality or the inherent dignity one possesses by the mere fact of being human.

Tom, on the other hand, knows that individuals cannot be explained (or "fixed") by science alone. Like Percy himself, Tom understands that the human being is comprised of intellect, emotion, creativity, and faith. He knows that medicine is not the answer to all social ills. And he inherently understands that you do not use science to solve problems that it does not even claim to be able to answer—such as: What does it mean to be human?

Tom is the one who exposes Comeaux and, with the help of his heroic cousin, the epidemiologist Dr. Lucy Lipscomb, eventually foils Project Blue Boy. But the prophet who pushes him to see the wider implications of Bob's insidious governmental activities is the ascetic Father Smith, a recovering alcoholic who lives alone in a forestry watch tower like a modern-day John the Baptist. When he was a young man, he tells Tom, he traveled to Nazi Germany where he encountered physicians and scientists, "cultured men dedicated to the betterment of humanity." It was these same "tenderhearted" men, he reflects, who gave medical sanction to the Holocaust.

Near the end of the novel, Fr. Smith preaches a hairraising sermon, proclaiming in part: "Beware, tender hearts! Don't you know where tenderness leads? To the gas chambers. Never in the history of the world have there been so many civilized tenderhearted souls as have lived in this century. Never in the history of the world have so many people been killed. More people have been killed in this century by tenderhearted souls than by cruel barbarians in all other centuries put together. My brothers, let me tell you where tenderness leads. To the gas chambers! On with the jets!"

Even a *good* such as tenderness, says the wise but eccentric Fr. Smith, can be perverted when it is removed from its basis in God's love for all, an insight that reminds one of the "tenderhearted" among us these days—say, Bill and Melinda Gates, Warren Buffet, or George Soros, whose self-proclaimed love of humanity, wholly separated as it is from the love of Christ, results in a narrow, sectarian, inwardly focused philanthropy that enables abortion, euthanasia, population control, mass vaccinations of whole populations, and other 21st-century equivalents of the gas chamber. Like Bob Comeaux, our contemporary human-itarians engage in vigorous eugenics work, which they defend and the world largely accepts on the grounds of social well-being and compassion for suffering. Like Bob Comeaux, they do not see themselves in relationships with the people they claim to want to help.

Perhaps the most important question raised by *The Thanatos Syndrome* is whether it's ever appropriate to change human nature, even if ostensibly for the sake of improving the quality of life for a great many people. Tom More presents a compelling iconoclastic argument that it isn't. Although Walker Percy died before the advent of the most radical advocates of remaking human nature—transhu-manists and extropians—this his final novel satirizes the grand solutions that they would come to propose in the following decades. In doing so, he prompts us to reflect upon themes of personal healing, moral good, and hope in the "age of thanatos."

The Wanting Seed (1962)
ANTHONY BURGESS

*A*nthony Burgess is best known for *A Clockwork Orange*, his nightmarish 1962 novella in which the "ultra-violent" teenage Alex narrates his nocturnal exploits, providing lengthy descriptions of heinous crimes perpetrated by his gang of wilding thugs in a Britain of the near future. Stanley Kubrick popularized Burgess's novella in his 1971 film, which became a cult classic. Nevertheless, *The Wanting Seed*, Burgess's overlooked novel published the same year as *A Clockwork Orange*, is far more enduring in its dystopian prescience; in fact, it would be an understatement to suggest that this Malthusian tragicomedy depicts a world terrifyingly familiar to the 21st-century reader.

Burgess imagines a future formed by the ideology of overpopulation alarmism—and it's grim. Tristram Foxe, *The Wanting Seed*'s hapless protagonist, is a self-described Augustinian living in a Pelagian world. A history teacher at an all-boys high school, Tristram is introduced as he is being denied his long-awaited promotion to chairman of his department. His principal explains that what gets a man a job these days is not his qualifications, not how many degrees he's got, nor how good he is at whatever it is he does. It's his "family background," a euphemism that refers to his marital status and the number of children he has. "You're entitled to marry if you want to," the principal informs him. "You're entitled to one birth in the family, though of course the best people just don't."

Tristram has no living children of his own, his wife's one allotted birth having ended in an infant death at the hands of doctors who are loathe to save a sick child because it means one more burden for society and one additional drain on the common good. "You just don't seem to care about human life any more. Any of you," charges Tristram's wife, Beatrice-Joanna, whose son has just died in hospital. "We care about stability," retorts the attending physician (in a literary hat tip to the World State from Aldous Huxley's *Brave New World*). "We care about not letting the earth get overrun." And then the doctor warns her: "Try to stop feeling like a mother. You've had your recommended ration. No more motherhood for you." On her way out of the hospital, the grieving Beatrice-Joanna must pass anti-mothering propaganda posters ("Don't Have Any More!") put out by the Department of Contraceptive Research. Other posters encourage women to "further reduce their bustline" in order to rid the female body of its motherly aspects.

Burgess, writing in the early 1960s, presaged China's draconian one-child policy, which the Central Committee of the Communist Party instituted in 1980, ostensibly to counter a devastating food shortage and famine. One-child families were rewarded—couples who abided were given a "Certificate of Honor for Single-Child Parents"—while parents with more than one child were humiliated, fined, and, in some cases, imprisoned. Though the Western world didn't exactly follow suit, anti-child campaigns in most countries—especially in the United States, which chose to follow the Margaret Sanger script from 1973 onward—were highly successful in propagandizing the idea of limiting family size as a means to being "socially responsible." To this day in many parts of the country, it is difficult to deny that large families still scandalize the average American Dick and Jane. In other words, as Burgess predicted, fecundity would be attacked on grounds that it's an offense against the interests of a healthy society.

But back to Tristram, who, of course, is also grieving the death of his only child. Despite Tristram's loss and lack of living progeny, his boss, principal of the South London Unitary School for Boys, explains that the promotion will go instead to one of Tristram's younger and less-experienced colleagues, an overt homosexual who has duly thumbed his nose at human fecundity. "The homos, remember, virtually run this country and, for that matter, the whole of the English-Speaking Union," the principal reminds Tristram.

These two conversations—Tristram's with his principal, and Beatrice-Joanna's with her doctor—encapsulate the idiosyncrasies of Burgess's dystopian world, and everything else flows directly from these two core values: Bearing children is irresponsible—having "a family pattern of deliberate fertility," Tristram's boss explains, is "like being a hereditary criminal"—and homosexuality is a lauded subversion of nature. In fact, the principal puts Tristram on notice, warning him that, should his wife become pregnant for a second time, he will be sacked without further consideration.

Divorce and homosexualization is the preferred route for those who wish to ascend the academic ladder. And when the homosexualized educators are teaching and mentoring the youth, guess what tends to be promoted? Homosexuality, of course, and anything else that diverts sex from its natural end. All over the school (and beyond), posters put out by the Ministry of Infertility (a hat tip to George Orwell's *Nineteen Eighty-Four*) depict a pair of males embracing each other with the legend "It's Sapiens to be Homo" or "Love Your Fellow-Men."

One of the most unfortunate byproducts of this form of indoctrination is an accompanying attitude of disdain for women and fertility. It stands to reason that when the values of society are built on a foundation of anti-woman, population-control alarmism, the result is brutish. Because traditional family life in Burgess's dystopia can result in loss of respect, human dignity, and professional advancement, many of the men masquerade as homosexuals, imitating the stereotypical lisp and manners of the effete and effeminate. Beatrice-Joanna, for example, encounters "a foppish steatopygous young man" in the elevator who begins "with swift expert strokes to make up his face, simpering, as his lips kissed the lipstick at his reflection in the lift mirror," all while looking down on Beatrice-Joanna and the other women in the elevator. Before you go looking up steatopygous in the dictionary, the word derives from the Greek, meaning tallow (stéar) rump (pugḗ), in other words, according to denotation, "having extreme accumulation of fat tissue on the buttocks and thighs, a build not confined to the gluteal regions, but extending to the outside and front of the thighs, and tapering to the knee," producing the kind of curvaceous figure found ironically in the fertility statues of Pre-Columbian cultures. And foppish? That's a dude who has the characteristics of a fop, that 17th-century dandy who was excessively concerned with his clothes and physical appearance, often resorting to powdering his nose, rouging his cheeks, and plucking his eyebrows. Thus, the "foppish steatopygous" fellow in the elevator exemplifies the kind of anti-fecund male the government means to elevate. Of course, the fact that this tallow-rumped man looks condescendingly on real women is indicative of the prevailing attitude toward potential motherhood.

To put this elevator vignette into its proper ironic perspective: Here we have a man who, masquerading as a woman—he even goes so far as to alter his body shape with injected adipose tissue—looks disdainfully at real women, perhaps envious of their natural, God-given feminine beauty and fecundity. The astute 21st-century reader sits up straight. "Wait!" he exclaims. "This seems

eerily familiar!" Given this century's glorification of vasec-
tomy, tubal ligation, cosmetic surgery, transsexualism, and
transgenderism, indeed it ought to seem familiar.

In Burgess's society, it's not always clear who is actually homosexual—those, that is, authentically attracted to
members of the same sex—and who is merely playing the
part. The masquerader, in order to get ahead in the world,
is "perpetually acting a public part, owing his position,
his chance of promotion, to the gross lie" that he is a
homosexual. In fact, Beatrice-Joanna's furtive lover, Derek,
who happens to be Tristram's brother, mimes orthodox
homosexual behavior, wearing a public skin of dandified
epicene, in order to advance his political career and to
provide cover for his extracurricular activities with a fecund
female. When it is later discovered by political rivals that
Derek has a heterosexual lover, he's exposed and expunged.

So, what happens to the poor mother who conceives a
child after her single government-rationed birth, a woman
who has an "illicit pregnancy"? Burgess uses Beatrice-
Joanna's story to explain. When she happily discovers her
second pregnancy—unsure if the baby is her husband's
or her lover's—she begins a life on the run from the
black vans of the Population Police ("the PoPo") as society
continues to degenerate due to the government's increasingly dehumanizing anti-woman, anti-child policies. This
spiraling dehumanization leads first to poverty, then to
famine, and, ultimately, to cannibalism. Yes, citizens, in
their state of amoral despair, begin to eat one another.

The first we hear of this is the story of little Jim Whittle
who didn't come to school one day because his parents
"cut him up and ate him"—at once feeding themselves and
doing their civic duty to alleviate poverty and overpopulation (a hat tip to "A Modest Proposal for Preventing
the Children of Poor People from Being a Burden to
Their Parents or Country," Jonathan's Swift's satirical
1729 tract proposing that impoverished Irish parents sell

their one-year-old children to their English overlords to be roasted and eaten, and their skin tanned to make leather gloves). Burgess's society arguably descends even further than that. Cannibalism in *The Wanting Seed* eventually becomes de rigueur as starving people set up public "dining clubs." A man named Thomas Wharton, for example, was heading home from work one night when he was set upon by starving young hooligans: "These knifed him, stripped him, spitted him, basted him, carved him, served him—all openly and without shame in one of the squares of the town."

Where is God in all this? It will probably come as no surprise that the vast majority of citizens in Burgess's dystopia have rejected the Judeo-Christian God as a "tragic conception," most never having even set eyes on a Bible, let alone having read the Word. The pope, "an old, old man," has been banished, as was Napoleon, to the island of St. Helena. Underground priests, the few who still remain, are rounded up and jailed for preaching morality and especially for denouncing the Sin of Sodom. Just as Henry Ford absurdly replaced Our Lord in Huxley's *Brave New World*, in Burgess's dystopia the Bible has been replaced by The Adventures of Mr. Livedog, fictional "cosmicomics" construed to brainwash the masses into believing the overpopulation scare: "Mr. Livedog was a big funny fubsy demiurge who, sufflaminandus like Shakespeare, spawned unwanted life all over earth. Overpopulation was his doing. In none of his adventures, however, did he ever win: Mr. Homo, his human boss, always brought him to heel." (It's likely no coincidence that "livedog" is "god evil" backwards.)

Yet, curiously, once society degenerates to the point of cannibalism, the pendulum begins to swing away from Pelagianism and back to Augustinianism. Eventually, the government overlords become so frightened by the world they have created that they're even willing to let Catholic priests resume celebrating Mass—openly and legally—the

way a desperate farmer might seek the help of a sha-
man rainmaker to bring water to his parched and failing
crops. Their Pelagian society turns out to have been little
more than a massive Frankensteinian experiment, one
that threatens to devour its creators. And that calls for
desperate measures—like praying to the one true God and
celebrating the Holy Sacrifice of the Mass.

Admittedly, *The Wanting Seed* becomes absurdist to the
point of slapstick burlesque at this juncture in the story,
and it likely appeared even more so when the novel first
appeared in 1962. Sixty years later, however, The Adventures of Mr. Livedog, lipstick-wearing men, sex changes,
and overzealous population controllers don't seem as much
absurd as frighteningly quotidian. After all, in the 21st century, we glorify same-sex marriage and gay pride, women
are more likely than not to be contracepting or sterilized,
abortion is regarded as a legal right, aborted babies are
sold for their body parts, and children may decide for
themselves whether to undergo a sex change before they
are old enough to buy cigarettes, vote, or drink a beer.

As in *The Wanting Seed*, all these 21st-century trends flow
from a Pelagian philosophy, articulated well in the novel
by Tristram Foxe. Pelagius, he explains, was a heretical
monk who "denied the Doctrine of Original Sin and said
that man was capable of working out his own salvation." A
government functioning in its Pelagian phase, he instructs
his inattentive high school students early in the novel,
commits itself to the belief that "man is perfectible, that
perfection can be achieved by his own efforts, and that
the journey towards perfection is along a straight road.
Man wants to be perfect." The problem, however, is that
the Pelagian powers-that-be become disappointed when
they find that men are not as good as they thought they
were; it then becomes necessary to force the citizens into
goodness. "The laws are reasserted," explains Tristram, "a
system of enforcement of those laws is crudely and hastily

knocked together. Disappointment opens up a vista of chaos. There is irrationality, there is panic. When the reason goes, the brute steps in.... Beatings-up. Secret police. Torture in brightly lighted cellars. Condemnation without trial. Fingernails pulled out with pincers. The rack. The cold-water treatment. The gouging-out of eyes. The firing squad in the cold dawn." This is the syllabus for a godless world, a world bent on denying reality, undermining nature, and promoting sin. It was the syllabus for much of the 20th century, and, without proper correctives like a restoration of reality, an assent to God, and an acknowledgment of Original Sin, it may be the same story for the 21st century—or worse.

"William Wilson" (1839)

EDGAR ALLAN POE

"*Y*ou have conquered, and I yield," admits William Wilson's doppelganger to the protagonist of the eponymous Edgar Allan Poe short story. "Yet, henceforward art thou also dead—dead to the World, to Heaven and to Hope! In me didst thou exist—and, in my death, see by this image, which is thine own, how utterly thou hast murdered thyself." After years of being dogged by a lookalike who attempts to thwart his every sin, William Wilson stabs to death this life-long rival whom he calls "scoundrel! impostor! accursed villain!" The rival has pursued him from his school days on to university and into his adulthood travels throughout Europe and Egypt. But William Wilson's doppelganger, who looks and dresses exactly as William Wilson himself, is no mere stalker; rather, Poe uses this doppelganger motif as a physical manifestation of Wilson's conscience and ultimately shows the demise of a man who, being blinded by his sins, kills his own conscience.

The troubled Poe explored the concepts of conscience, guilt, remorse, and the consequences of sin in a number of his short stories, most famously perhaps in "The Tell-tale Heart," the brief and simple narrative of a man's guilty conscience leading him to confess that he's killed a man and buried his body beneath his floorboards and to turn himself in to the authorities, if only to stop the panic caused by his conscience accusing him. The protagonist in Poe's "William Wilson" takes another path: He spends his life running from his conscience and its counsels to stick to the straight and narrow. Wilson himself narrates the story in retrospect, setting down his account as a kind of oblique cautionary tale and a plea for sympathy from his fellow man as he nears the grave. The ultimate message: disregard your conscience at your own peril.

Born into a 19th-century noble English family, William Wilson's "weak-minded" parents could do little to check the evil propensities of his childhood years. Some "feeble and ill-directed efforts" result in complete failure on their part and a total triumph for him. "At an age when few children have abandoned their leading strings, I was left to the guidance of my own will," admits Wilson, "and became, in all but name, the master of my own action." Even before he enters school, William Wilson grows self-willed, addicted to the wildest caprices, and prey to the most ungovernable passions—a true problem child with little regard for anyone but himself.

Once Wilson reaches the age of reason, his parents send him away to be educated at one of England's finest boarding schools. Other than providing Wilson with an allowance that enables him to live in ridiculous luxury, they contribute little to his upbringing or to his moral formation. Significantly, Wilson meets his doppelganger on the day he enters boarding school at Dr. Bransby's Academy in a sheltered misty village with deep-shadowed avenues evoking classic Poe gothic. His imperiousness and self-will earns him an ascendency over all the other students not greatly older than himself—with one exception. A boy with the same name, the same birthdate, and the same physical features fast becomes what Wilson regards as his rival: "My namesake alone presumed to ... refuse implicit belief in my assertions, and submission to my will—indeed to interfere with my arbitrary dictation in any respect whatsoever." In other words, the rival William Wilson is the only person unwilling to submit to the

narrator Wilson's will. And the narrator admits to himself
that he believes this is proof of his rival's superiority. He's
too young to realize it at this point in his life, but what
he is recognizing is moral superiority.

Although the two are lookalikes, the rival Wilson has
one significant physical difference: He can speak no
louder than a whisper due to damaged vocal chords. This
whispering doppelganger increasingly interferes with the
narrator's will, especially when Wilson is committing sin.
Although the point is lost on Wilson, the implication is
obvious to the reader: this whispering rival who interferes
with William Wilson's will—especially when he sets out
to contravene the moral law—is a manifestation of the
narrator's conscience, perhaps a heaven-sent guardian
with designs on redeeming this poor soul.

William Wilson eventually moves on to the famous
Eton College in Windsor for the next stage of his education. Glad to be rid of his namesake's constant whispering
admonishments, he descends into a thoughtless vortex of
folly and debauchery. For three years he leads this life of
"soulless dissipation," in which a number of vices become
inveterate. Abetted by his parents' endless flow of money,
Wilson establishes himself as a miserable profligate living
in what he calls "delirious extravagance." Then one night
in the waning hours of an orgy-like party, Wilson's doppelganger, dressed precisely as Wilson, enters his apartment
uninvited. Before the narrator can comprehend what's
happening, the rival Wilson seizes his arm and whispers
the words "William Wilson!" in his ear before turning on
his heels to depart as suddenly as he appeared. Startled
by this solemn admonition, the narrator sobers up immediately, recalling his schoolboy days with his namesake.
But, perhaps because his inveterate sins have eclipsed his
reason, William Wilson is unable or unwilling to heed the
doppelganger's implicit warning.

Soon thereafter he makes his way to Oxford for his

university studies. And, instead of maturing intellectually or emotionally, William Wilson compounds his moral turpitude by becoming a vile gambler and cardsharp. He is no longer content with his parents' enormous allowance that allows him to out-Herod Herod (as he explains); he sets out to financially ruin one of Oxford's wealthiest students, a young parvenu nobleman by the name of Lord Glendinning. Without going into the unnecessary details, suffice it to say that William Wilson had by now developed a long con cardsharping scheme. He lures Glendinning into some late-night gambling, and in a very short period the unwitting nobleman finds himself deeply in debt to Wilson. As the night wears on, that debt doubles and then quadruples—in front of a room of witnesses. At the point when Glendinning realizes that he has lost everything, Wilson's doppelganger arrives on the scene, unexpected and unannounced. Again, he is dressed exactly as William Wilson, a point which spooks the narrator. But this time he is not there to simply admonish the narrator; this time the whispering Wilson exposes the narrator's cheating scheme to the roomful of witnesses. The host of the party, who hadn't known anything of Wilson's cardsharping skills and designs, searches William Wilson's pockets and finds, just as the rival Wilson has indicated, extra cards up his sleeves. Glendinning is saved and William Wilson is forced to leave Oxford under the shroud of scandal.

From there, William Wilson flees to continental Europe, hoping he can escape what he comes to regard as his archenemy and tormentor. But in every city, at every turn, the rival is there to thwart his sinful undertakings: "my ambition at Rome, my revenge at Paris, my passionate love at Naples, or what he falsely termed my avarice in Egypt." These pursuits continue for years until Wilson the narrator decides he's had enough. At Rome, during the extravagant debauchery of Italy's Carnival week, Wilson attends a masquerade ball at the palazzo of Duke Di Broglio where he intends to keep a secret assignation with the duke's young, beautiful, but unscrupulous wife. As he is making his way excitedly into her presence, Wilson is stopped by a hand on his shoulder. It's the whispering rival Wilson once again, and he's dressed in the very same costume as the narrator, a stylized "Spanish cloak of blue velvet, begirt about the waist with a crimson belt sustaining a rapier. A mask of black silk entirely covered his face." Lechery giving way now to wrath, Wilson grabs his namesake by the collar and threatens, "You shall not dog me unto death!" In his fury, he pulls the rival Wilson into a private side room, away from the ballroom and there plunges his sword repeatedly through and through the bosom of his adversary. It is at this moment that, looking upon his rival, he sees himself—bleeding, dying. The doppelganger, speaking no longer in a whisper but in Wilson's own full voice, makes it clear that William Wilson, unable to submit to anyone's will but his own, has killed his conscience, and without a conscience, he'll have nothing to stop him from descending to the level of a beast. He is "dead to the World, to Heaven, and to Hope," he tells Wilson. "Without me, without your conscience, you are left to your own devices—and your own devices will lead you only to the darkest pits of hell for an eternity of suffering." All this, because William Wilson is unable to govern his passions, is unable to submit to anyone's will but his own. The only redemption, the only hope, it seems, is William Wilson's written confessional, the tale in which he features as the wayward protagonist, by which he hopes to garner his fellow man's sympathy. It is here where he seeks to explain that killing the rival Wilson, killing his conscience has led him to "unspeakable misery." William Wilson doesn't quite know it, but he's begging God (and man) for forgiveness—and in writing about his own journey to unspeakable misery, he succeeds in thwarting despair and, consequently, allowing the possibility of hope to lead him away from eternal misery.

Things Fall Apart (1958)
CHINUA ACHEBE

*C*hinua Achebe was writing about the "clash of civilizations" long before it was popularized by Samuel P. Huntington, when in 1993 he predicted that "conflict between civilizations will be the latest phase in the evolution of conflict in the modern world." Achebe, Nigeria's most highly acclaimed novelist, was born in Eastern Nigeria in 1930, during the era of colonial rule. His family belonged to the Ibo tribe, and even before his birth, representatives of the British government that controlled Nigeria convinced his parents to leave their tribal religion and convert to Christianity. Achebe himself was brought up as a Christian (his baptismal name is Albert), but he remained curious about the more traditional Nigerian faiths.

In 1958, Achebe published his first novel: *Things Fall Apart*. His groundbreaking masterpiece (and the first in a trilogy) centers on the clash of civilizations between his native Ibo culture and the influence of white Christian missionaries and the colonial government in Nigeria in the 1890s. In particular, it is the story of Okonkwo, a traditional Ibo warrior and yam farmer who is unable to adapt to changing conditions in the early days of British rule.

One could be forgiven for assuming that *Things Fall Apart* is a politically correct dramatization of all the evils perpetrated by white people on traditional black African culture. After all, the title itself, taken from a line in

W. B. Yeats's 1919 poem "The Second Coming," suggests that Christian missionaries devalued and devastated the Ibo way of life, causing a collapse of their society. Yes, in the end, we witness the traditional Ibos capitulate to a powerful new order. Yet, despite the many shortcomings of the British colonialists, this new order, grounded in European Judeo-Christian values and institutions, ushers in not chaos or collapse, but a revitalized way of living— especially in matters of justice, family life, and attitudes toward women and children. That's no popular message in the 21st century. Most of us were brought up to believe that the European colonials were mere evil-doers.

Achebe, whose parents and ancestors were of the Ibo tribe, in no way glamorizes their traditional tribal life. He chooses the complex Okonkwo as his protagonist, and it is through this tragic hero's words and deeds that Achebe introduces the world to the animist Ibo tribe, their religion, their values, and their brutally misogynistic way of life. Acclaimed throughout Umuofia's nine villages as a powerful wrestler and warrior (he's killed five men and has their heads as trophies to prove it), Okonkwo routinely beats his three wives, has little empathy for his children, and disrespects his own father for being a loafer and a debtor, but perhaps more importantly for his love of "gentleness"—seen by Ibo men as a distastefully feminine trait. And Okonkwo is by no means gentle.

An Ibo man earns tribal respect through his accumulation of wives, titles, human heads (yes, chopped off and displayed), and yams, the "man's crop" that allows one to support his family from one harvest to the next. Okonkwo has three wives, each with her own separate family hut, where she cooks for Okonkwo and raises her children. Only the first wife (who, it is instructive to note, is never even named) has anything approaching familial honors. The others are mere trophy wives, used primarily for sexual pleasure and as seedbeds for more children. Okonkwo, we are told, rules his household with a heavy hand: "His wives ... lived in perpetual fear of his fiery temper, and so did his little children." His youngest wife, Ojiugo, for example, provokes Okonkwo's anger when she goes to plait her hair at a friend's house but fails to return early enough to cook Okonkwo his afternoon meal. When Ojiugo returns to her hut, Okonkwo beats her mercilessly, even though his other two wives desperately plead with him to stop. "Okonkwo," we are told, "was not the man to stop beating someone half-way through." And so that we might not mistakenly suppose this wife-beating incident as anomalous, a few weeks later Okonkwo's second wife, Ekwefi, suffers her husband's violent temper. In this case, Okonkwo mistakenly believes Ekwefi to have killed his banana tree. Not interested in listening to his wife's explanation that she had merely trimmed the leaves and that the tree was still very much alive, "Okonkwo gave her a sound beating." After his anger is satisfied, he decides to go hunting with "an old rusty gun made by a clever blacksmith who had come to live in Umuofia long ago." Ekwefi, who has just been beaten, murmurs something about "guns that never shot." Unfortunately, Okonkwo hears the remark, loads his gun, and shoots at her as she is running away from him. Being a yam farmer and a machete warrior, his shot misses Ekwefi.

Not only does this scene with Ekwefi highlight the misogynistic wife-beating culture of the Ibo tribe, it showcases the tendency for the Ibos to act without justice. The innocent in this society suffer mercilessly and senselessly. Justice, classically identified by white European culture as one of the four cardinal virtues, has been called (by Plato et al.) "the first virtue of social institutions." Without justice, these social institutions—for example, marriage and the family—cannot properly flourish. Without the personal virtue of justice, the individual cannot flourish. Okonkwo regards his wives and children as little more than personal property, to be treated or mistreated as his whims desire—without regard to justice. If he believes his wife has killed one of his banana plants and refuses to listen to her explain the vital process of pruning, he takes it out on her with his fists; if he feels his pride is wounded by her mumbled words, he takes it out on her with a gun. In other words, Okonkwo acts on the philosophy that "might makes right"—the strong man does as he pleases, without taking into consideration the good of his marriage, his family, or the common welfare of society. Okonkwo—and he presumably represents the typically Ibo warrior male—considers only himself.

Judging from *Things Fall Apart*, Ibo society's general sense of justice fares no better. For example, the Ibo tribe seems to have no understanding of the concept of a natural justice, that the precepts of the natural moral law and the existence of natural rights determine what is just and unjust. In fact, even the idea of a natural moral law seems to them as foreign as the European colonialists. Throughout the novel, Ibo men, women, and children are routinely punished for what is beyond their control. From a reading of Achebe's novel, one might easily conclude that the Ibos punish the innocent (due to animist superstitions) more than they punish the guilty.

Okonkwo's father dies of a disease known to the Ibos as "the swelling." Though most men throughout history have no control of which disease takes their lives, according to Ibo culture, dying of "the swelling" is considered "an abomination to the earth goddess." Those who suffer from such a disease are not accorded a burial ("The sickness was an abomination to the earth, and so the victim could not be buried in her bowels"); rather, they are carried out into "the Evil Forest" to die and their bodies consumed by wild animals. But not only is it an abomination to die of certain diseases, in some Ibo villages it is also an abomination to die during the so-called "Week of Peace," the week preceding the planting of crops: "If a man dies at this time he is not buried but cast into the Evil Forest."

Not only is there no justice in Ibo death, there's no justice in Ibo birth. Born a twin? Too bad! The Ibos put newborn twins in earthenware pots and throw them away in the forest. And if your child should die as an infant or a young child, guess who's at fault? Yep, very possibly the infant. In the case of one of Ekwefi's children, the dead child was taken by the medicine man, who "brought out a sharp razor from the goatskin bag slung from his left shoulder and began to mutilate the child. Then he took it [the child] away to bury in the Evil Forest, holding it by the ankle and dragging it on the ground behind him." This would supposedly teach the child to "think twice before coming again" to torment the same mother. Oh yes, the Ibo's believe in reincarnation, typically living seven lives before becoming an ancestor once and for all. In fact, most miscarriages of justice in Ibo culture can be attributed to superstitions arising from their polytheist animism.

It is interesting to note that this systemic Ibo injustice also works against Okonkwo. Remember that old rusty gun that he fired at Ekwefi? Recall that Ekwefi mumbled about his guns not properly firing? That's pure foreshadowing. Later in the novel, Ezeudu, the oldest man in the village, dies. At Ezeudu's funeral, we are witness to the demonic-like chaotic proceedings: shouting, the violent beating of drums, brandishing and clanging of machetes, and the firing of guns and cannons. As fate would have it, Okonkwo's rusty old gun explodes and a piece of iron pierces the heart of Ezeudu's 16-year-old son. And, although this was an accidental killing, presumably beyond Okonkwo's control, he and his family are banished from the clan for seven years because "it was a crime against the earth to kill a clansman, and a man who committed it must flee the land." Once they flee, the villagers set fire to Okonkwo's houses, demolish all his dirt walls, kill all his animals, and destroy his barn: "It was the justice of the earth goddess, and they were merely her messengers."

Achebe spends the first two-thirds of his novel dramatizing the horrors and brutality of Ibo life, with its misogyny, injustice, and inequality, before the white missionaries arrive on the scene. At first it appears the white Europeans have simply brought with them a new kind brutality. Unfortunately for the Umuofian village of Abame, after seeing a white man arrive peaceably among them, they consult their Oracle, which the Ibos take very, very seriously as pronouncements from on high. The Oracle warns in no uncertain terms that "the strange man would break their clan and spread destruction among them." They take heed of their superstitions and kill the white man who had come to them in peace. That, of course, does not sit well with the Anglican missionaries. They retaliate a few weeks later by wiping out the entire village of Abame. Ironically, says one of the Ibo men, "A great evil has come upon their land as the Oracle had warned"; never mind that this had all transpired because of what the Oracle had said in the first place. No, the white missionaries are no saints, but most of them do seem driven by an authentic desire to bring the Gospel to those who have never had the opportunity to hear the Word of God. In fact, the destruction of Abame remains an anomalous retributive act, one that is acknowledged as clearly un-Christian.

During Okonkwo's seven years of banishment, many Ibo tribesman convert to Christianity, his oldest son Nwoye among them. The white missionaries begin their preaching with a simple Christian truth that many of the Ibo's find attractive: We are all sons of one God, and therefore we are all brothers and sisters. All men—European or African, white or black—will be judged before the same God when they die. "We have been sent by this great God," says one of the missionaries, "to ask you to leave your wicked ways and false gods and turn to Him so that you may be saved when you die."

Nwoye in particular is captivated by this preaching, by this theological view of the world, by this revelation of truth and natural moral law. At the same time he senses in his heart that his own religion is barbaric. Another early convert is a woman by the name of Nneka, who is pregnant when the white men arrive on the scene. She had four previous childbirths, each time delivering twins. Each time the twins, according to Ibo superstitious custom, had been immediately thrown away. Having already had to sacrifice eight children, Nneka understands that, as a Christian, the missionaries would welcome her children, if she were to give birth again to twins. Already the missionaries have begun rescuing discarded twins from "the Evil Forest." As for Nneka's family, they happily disown her since they had long dismissed her as cursed.

As for Okonkwo, he threatens to kill his son Nwoye with a heavy stick for his association with the Christians, whom Okonkwo regards as "effeminate men who cluck like chickens." Yet these Christians bring with them government and a justice system to protect the Christians, white and black. They bring with them a system of equality that accords all men, women, and children with the same basic human rights.

Certainly, conflict and division ensue as many Ibos convert while others refuse to submit, as they say, to the white man's culture. The remainder of the novel chronicles the clash of civilizations—and it certainly isn't always black and white. Nevertheless, Achebe deftly conveys the gifts of Christianity brought to this part of Nigeria in the late 19th century by less-than-perfect Anglican missionaries. Except for those intractable souls like Okonkwo, many of the Ibo tribesmen realize in the end that "even in the matter of religion there was a growing feeling that there might be something in it after all, something vaguely akin to method in the overwhelming madness."

MICHAEL S. ROSE is author of several previous books, including *Goodbye Good Men*, *Ugly As Sin*, and *Benedict XVI: The Man Who Was Ratzinger*. He holds degrees in Architecture (Cincinnati), Literary Arts (Brown), and Education (Xavier), as well as the Certificate of School Management and Leadership from Harvard Business School. From 2005 to 2021 he served as Book Editor and Associate Editor for *New Oxford Review*, in which some of these essays appeared in slightly different form as a part of his monthly "Literature Matters" column. He also taught literature, composition, journalism, and rhetoric at the college and high school levels before assuming his current position as Headmaster of Cincinnati Classical Academy. He is married with five children and lives in Cincinnati.